CONFESSIONS

OF A

VINTAGE GUITAR DEALER

CONFESSIONS

OF A

VINTAGE GUITAR DEALER

THE MEMOIRS OF
Norman Harris

NORMAN W. HARRIS

WITH

DAVID YORKIN

HAL LEONARD BOOKS
AN IMPRINT OF HAL LEONARD CORPORATION

Published in 2016 by Hal Leonard Books
An Imprint of Hal Leonard Corporation
7777 West Bluemound Road
Milwaukee, WI 53213

Trade Book Division Editorial Offices
33 Plymouth St., Montclair, NJ 07042

Printed in the United States of America

Book design by Michael Kellner

Library of Congress Cataloging-in-Publication Data

Names: Harris, Norman W., 1949- author. | Yorkin, David, author.
Title: Confessions of a vintage guitar dealer : the memoirs of Norman Harris
  / Norman W. Harris, David Yorkin.
Description: Milwaukee, WI : Hal Leonard Books, 2016.
Identifiers: LCCN 2015043844 | ISBN 9781495035111 (hardcover)
Subjects: LCSH: Harris, Norman W., 1949- | Guitar–Collectors and collecting.
  | Businessmen–United States–Biography. | Guitar–United States–History.
Classification: LCC ML1015.G9 H285 2016 | DDC 787.87/19092–dc23
LC record available at http://lccn.loc.gov/2015043844

www.halleonardbooks.com

To Marlene, the love of my life, who's stuck around through it all, from the ridiculous to the sublime. My success is directly attributed to you.

Also to my son, Jordan, my daughter, Sarah, and her husband, Troy, my granddaughter, Brooklyn, and my grandson, Oliver.

Contents

CONTENTS

Foreword

D edication to Norm—
So, let me introduce you to Norman Harris. I think the first time I walked into Norm's shop was 1988. I had just made a little money so I could afford to walk into his store. It was a small spot on the corner of Tampa and Vanowen Streets in Reseda. I had been hanging around with Cher and her son, Elijah Allman, who was getting to know the guitar. I was giving him a little bit of a hand, and I said, "Let's go down and see this rare guitar shop," which I'd heard great things about but had never been there. When we got there, I met Norman. He was gracious enough to let us play some instruments that he knew I couldn't afford. Then he gave me a really good deal on things that were appropriate for my income bracket. It was very, very nice of him. When you believe in doing that for a musician, you give him an opportunity to grow to the next level, and that is very important.

It was at that moment I knew that Norm and I were friends; we could talk to each other in a language that we both understood.

Lord knows, he was very lenient to me in the lean years, and I love him for that. He knows that when it comes to a starter kit of your first vintage axe, you'll fall in love and never fall out.

So thank you, Norm. I'm a junkie now, a vintage guitar junkie, and it's all your fault, but that is a healthy habit. All I know is, when you walk into Norm's store, it's like heaven. At any given time you know you're going to fall in love four or five times before you leave, and the interesting part about that is you're almost walking back in time, because the instruments you can acquire are timeless. So you'd better bring your checkbook.

———————

Norm has helped a tremendous amount of musicians reach their goals through supplying them with the instruments to hone their craft. He understands a musician's needs and that's no easy task. Guess what, Norm? That's it!

I don't know if you know this but Norm is quite an accomplished musician himself. Norman is a Hammond organ specialist who has played with numerous top musicians. He has backed up Little Richard, Bo Didley, Dobie Gray, and Albert Collins on many occasions, as well as Lowell Fulsom, Eddie "Clean Head" Vinson, Roy Milton, Big Mama Thornton, and numerous other iconic bluesmen and women. He has had songs in several movies. He currently has a song on John Legend's latest album and has even had a huge hit with the rapper Common.

Supplying dreams is something else amazing about Norm. You walk into his store or call him and he says, "What do you need to fulfill that dream?" So you tell him what it is, and he says, "I got it, *I got it!*" You know that's a very special thing. Then he'll call you up at any moment, out of the blue, and say, "You need this guitar, Rich, this is for you, and this is your guitar." Norm and I have a relationship that spans almost thirty years, so he knows me, the player, and he knows me, the person. 'Cause it ain't about the money for him. I mean, let's face it. Everyone must make a living. He's a musician, and it's a pleasure for him to see all the musicians he knows flourish, prosper, and make a living playing music, especially with a guitar. That's Norm.

He's the vintage guitar pusher, because he knows you'll become addicted. I say that in the best of ways.

When you give a musician the right instrument, it's a very important day in his or her life, like an angel has come down and tapped him
on the shoulder with the right wand. Norm does that every day. Music
has been my life for as long as I can remember; it's my sanctuary, my
church, and a source of spirituality for me. Whenever I take the stage,
whether it's in front of seventy people or a stadium filled with seventy
thousand people, it is the guitars that Norm has bestowed on me that I
use to light the candles on the altar of spirituality.

Norm's vibe is one at the heart and soul of a musician. He inher-
ently understands each musician's needs at his or her present level of
development. His extreme knowledge of these fine instruments is rare.
He is a master of knowing what instrument to put in the hands of which
musician and how they will both be best served.

Norm is the guy who granted me that 1959 Les Paul and a Broadcaster when I needed it, and then he'd call me up and, lo and behold, I
have a Strat No. 13. His instruments are not only rare in their being but
also in tone and work. They stay in tune, and as a professional musician, you have to have instruments that work.

If you work with Norm, he never misses your birthday, and when
you need a break, he'll give it to you. Norm gives deep from the heart
and never speaks of it or boasts.

Over the thirty years that we've known each other, I have known
him as a wonderful husband to Marlene and an amazing father to Jordan and Sarah (and now he's a granddad, HAH!). He's just a few years
older than me (I just started a little later).

Norm has been a mentor to me by sharing his knowledge, his love,
and his friendship, and also his endless philanthropic quest.

A few years back, my buddy Norm and my dear friend, assistant, and
right arm, Denise Smith-Salazar, began collaborating on a project. They
wanted to produce a three-show benefit concert series at the Malibu

Performing Arts Center to raise money for The Midnight Mission (LA's premier homeless shelter). They invited me to lend a hand in the most obvious way by asking, "Will you perform?" I said, "Of course!"

This was my introduction to the incredible body of work being done by The Midnight Mission, and Norm's dedication resonated with me. So, for over a decade, I've been humbled and proud to support the Mission however I can, and it's been one of the most rewarding experiences, more than anything else I've done in my life. Thank you, Norman.

Let's not forget the acoustics! Bring cash or trades if you're holdin'. The Martins and the Gibsons and the Epiphones that I use on every record that I make are the cornerstone of my tone, and I got them from Norm.

When Norman gets to know you and drops his guard he's like one big, open heart. He would do anything for you. I'm sure reading the stories in this book, you'll gain a lot of insight about the man that resides in Norm's body, it's Norman!

I'm writing this as I'm walking out of my house to go to my gig with my trusty 1938 Martin 000-42 that I've now played on countless albums . . . (yes, I'm sure since I've had it, it has gone up incredibly in value). Yes, brother, I'll buy you a car someday . . . probably already have. Every time I pick up any of the amazing instruments that I have gotten from Norm, I know they have become an appendage that I can rely on in any situation, in the studio or on the stage.

So now that I'm done masturbating your ego . . .

Norm,

You are family to me, and your family is family to me, and your family loves my family and mine, yours.

So enough of that . . . Love you much, bro and "don't stop shakin' the tree."

Enjoy the book.

—*Richie Sambora*

Preface

What is it about vintage guitars that fascinate collectors so much? Is it the feel, the craftsmanship, the sound, the backstory, or the desire to find the guitar that was made "just for you" . . . even before you knew it existed? If the answer to all these is yes, chances are you already have *it*. And what is *it*, you may ask? *It* . . . is the disease. The collecting bug and the willingness to go without food, clothing, or shelter to finance the next guitar or amp that you don't really need but have convinced yourself that it is now the "best guitar/amp I ever played/heard." A healthy addiction to vintage guitars and amps consumes every spare thought and action you have vis-à-vis your daily life and responsibilities. If you are a member of multiple discussion forums and have guitar-themed coffee mugs, house keys, T-shirts, and point-of-purchase memorabilia littered anywhere you can put it, you definitely have the disease. If you are married, there is normally a room dedicated to your addiction. And there you are, sequestered into your "man cave," surrounded by items that many who enter may not understand. But you do! Is your idea of heaven cranking up a Tweed Deluxe rather than a beach in Tahiti? Sound familiar? The "disease," this is the disease that has enriched my life ever since I bought a copy of Tom Wheeler's *American Guitars* book and saw Dan Toler play a Sunburst Les Paul with the Gregg Allman Band circa 1983. It was in those days that I began to truly fall in love with electric guitars primarily made in the mid- to late-fifties. My whole life has been transformed by the love of vintage guitars and amps and the pursuit of the knowledge of the manufacturers and the inventors behind the scenes. It is so fascinating that (even in modern times) most of the guitar-buying community is obsessed with designs and technology that were developed back in the thirties, forties, fifties, and sixties. Think about it. What other industry uses antiquated quarter-inch Switchcraft connectors as the industry standard? Imagine if the automotive industry only made cars like they did in the fifties? It would be like living in Cuba! A world frozen in time. However, for the guitar player of today, the guitar design and technology of the past cannot seem to be improved upon, and these relics of yesteryear are all standard fare in the guitar community of today.

I am the son of a guitar dealer and music store owner. I was raised in upstate New York in the late seventies and eighties, where there was a wonderful little circuit of clubs that had bands playing every Friday and Saturday night into the wee hours. Add to this, the drinking age was eighteen at the time and this combination fueled a music scene that was vibrant enough for one to make a decent living playing Bob Seger covers on the weekends. In the early eighties, there was a ton of used, vintage, and new guitar equipment for sale in a bevy of mom-and-pop music stores that stayed in business by serving the local music community. This meant that you could find an old Les Paul guitar and a Fender tube amp and still have enough for dinner from your $1,000 bank withdrawal. My father was one of those musicians who loved to buy and sell guitars even before he turned it into a business. Always seeking better guitars, there were many deals being made and a lot of "I need to sell this to pay for that." Being young and impressionable, I quickly learned from my father how cool it was to find something that had been hidden in a closet untouched for thirty years and learn its backstory. I learned how to turn one guitar into two by trading up. My dad would answer all the local classified ads that had any potential and I often got to go along with him on these "guitar safaris" because, like him, I was now addicted to the search for the illusive grails of guitar-dom. It was like a treasure hunt, and the best part was that we could make music with the things we found.

The Bonamassas never had a lot of money, and we lived a modest middle-class life, so it wasn't like we could buy everything we found on sight. My dad would always say, "If the bills are paid and the heat works then we can justify $300 on this chocolate-colored Princeton amp, but if times get tough, we will have to sell it." I always understood that and respected my father's practical approach to collecting. The "hunt" be-came a true bonding experience for father and son. I loved the guitars and amps we found, and I was into *it* in a big way.

I remember the first time I held a spaghetti logo'd Fender Stratocast-er in my hands that we had found during a weekend outing together. It was like I had been handed a Stradivarius violin. To Leo Fender, it was probably just a means to an end, but to me it was like Excalibur. I think I stared at it longer than I played it. To this very day I am a sucker for a Buddy Holly Strat. I mean . . . we are talking life-changing stuff here!

I met Norman around 1991 when I was flown out to Los Angeles to appear on the short-lived *Into the Night with Rick Dees* late night ABC program. I was part of a skit involving sixties rock-and-roll staple Billy Vera and a Barney Fife impersonator. That is all I will say on that matter. Anyway, during this trip to California my mom and my sister Lindsay decided to go sightseeing while my dad and I ventured off to discover the wonderful vintage guitar scene that was thriving in Los Angeles at the time. In 1991, both sides of Sunset Boulevard between Gardner and La Brea was packed with guitar shops full of old amps and guitars. It was sensory overload for this wide-eyed youth from upstate New York, and I remember vividly walking into these stores and seeing guitars that I had only seen in books. I particularly remember being yelled at by Lloyd Chiate at Voltage Guitars on Gardener Street for touching a tweed Deluxe he had on display. It was traumatizing at the time, but I came to learn it was a common occurrence at his shop. I remember my manager telling us of a shop in the valley called Norm's Rare Guitars. He said that this was the best vintage shop in Los Angeles. So after shaking off my scolding and my severe case of overstimulation (including a quick lunch at El Compadre), we drove out to Norm's for the very first time. This was the smaller shop before the Northridge earthquake. I will never forget that first visit. I was a nobody kid on his first trip to the "sunny place for shady people," and Norm was this kind, generous, and passionate soul who broke out the good stuff even for a twelve-year-old on a $2 a week allowance. I always remembered that. He didn't have to take the time with me and show me these beautiful guitars but he did, and I am very grateful for that. (BTW . . . he still has the signed eight-by-ten that I gave him that day . . . scary!)

I am really excited about this new book Norman is writing because it's all based on the stories of how he found many of his guitars and the people behind the scenes. There is no one on this planet who has owned more cool guitars than Norm. He had then (and still has now) the best guitars in the world. That now-infamous guitar collection scene in Spinal Tap says it all. The best of the best . . . oh and . . . that surf green Fender Bass VI . . . don't even look at it.

May the music be loud and the guitars "straight."

—*Joe Bonamassa*

P.S. Norm . . . on a side note, I wanted to let you know that I'm honored to write this for you and even more honored to call you my friend.

Acknowledgments

There have been so many people who have had an impact on me, but my late father, William Harris, leads the list. As the years go on, his words of wisdom and values loom large in my consciousness. Even though he passed away when I was sixteen years old, his business advice crosses my mind every day. He was larger than life itself. A close second is my wonderful late mom, Frances Harris, who believed in me even when it seemed all evidence pointed to the contrary. I am eternally grateful to my mother-in-law, Anne Kain, who helped me out countless times when I got into a financial jam. I also need to credit my wonderful staff who keep things running through thick and thin: Mark Agnesi, the talented Jen Angkahan, who did most of the photography and the cover photo for my book, Nick Dias, Joel Whitehead, and John Tucci. Much appreciation goes to Denise Salazar, my partner in all of my shows for The Midnight Mission and the hardest worker I know. Likewise for Georgia Berkovich of The Midnight Mission and all the good people that work at the Mission. I need to offer a shout-out to my reliable driver Frankie D. "Deluxe," Petey, the ever-constant Mario, and our excellent guitar teachers, Sal, Lorrie, and Bray.

———

I would also like to thank my two brothers, Emanuel and Jack, Manny's late wife, Rosa, for her belief in me, Jack's wife, Joni, my brother-in-law

ACKNOWLEDGMENTS

Alan Kornbluh, and his wife, Stephanie, and all my nieces and nephews and their children. This book wouldn't exist without the inspiration and knowledge so generously imparted to me by Bobby Caldwell and Bobby Jabo. I would like to thank my old Florida buddies, Tom Petty, Ron Blair, and the Heartbreakers. My good friend Jason Sinay, a great musician with a very big heart, who has helped The Midnight Mission in so many ways. Also my friends David Kalt and Scott Silver. I also want to acknowledge my buddies Rick G., Rick K., Jeff K., Chris T., Larry L., Brian M., Hank R., King Cotton, Robben Ford, and John 5. My good friends Richie Sambora and Joe Bonamassa, I can't thank you enough for doing the forewords to my book and for being the good friends that you have been over so many years. I'd like to also thank Mac Yasuda, Zen Yoshida, Masa Kondo, and all my friends from Japan. To the Karma Dealers, Mike and Shannon, thank you. Lastly to all the people who have worked for me in the past; to all my past bandmates; and to all the customers who have become friends over the years and have enriched my life through it all. To all the people who have ever bought or sold a guitar at Norman's Rare Guitars, thank you all!

Introduction

LET'S MAKE A DEAL

The late sixties and early seventies were a bleak time for American instrument manufacturing. The guitar boom had been going full throttle for a number of years. Guitar-driven music had taken over the charts and the radio. The market blew up. Every kid was learning how to play "Johnny B. Goode," and they needed guitars to play.

In trying to grab a piece of this action, almost all the big guitar companies made bad decisions about their products in pursuit of the bottom line. CBS bought Fender and Norlin bought Gibson, and the new corporate bosses proceeded to cut costs and increase production to build sales. Even the respected hundred-year-old family-owned C. F. Martin Company made cost-cutting decisions that negatively affected the quality of their instruments.

If you're reading this book, you're probably familiar with the lousy reputations of the guitars of the seventies. It was the era of three-bolt neck plates, pencil necks, giant rosewood bridge plates, inferior wood, cheap tuners, and poor quality control. If you haven't heard these terms, you can just go onto the Internet and research it all—in fact, you can find out everything you've ever wanted to know and become an "expert" overnight.

But back then, nobody knew anything.

Nobody except the musicians, that is.

It was an inside thing. The general public didn't know. But the hip players knew the old guitars just played better and sounded better. They would settle for nothing less. I knew this, because I was one of them. I sang and played keyboards, but I spent most of my waking hours with guitar players and bass players, while I played in bands and pursued music for many years.

But I'm getting ahead of myself in this story.

═══════

When I got into this game in the late sixties, the vintage market didn't even exist. We were making up the rules on the fly, discovering things along the way, sucking up every piece of information we could find, sometimes sharing it and sometimes not. There were no price guides, no Internet. I'd try to learn things from every source I could find, from the musicians, to pawn shops, to old repair guys who'd been fixing guitars for years. The first book to acknowledge the vintage guitar phenomenon was *American Guitars* by Tom Wheeler. There was also the "Rare Bird" column in *Guitar Player* magazine written by Robb Lawrence, but this only profiled one guitar per issue. That was it!

Over the years, as my business grew and the vintage guitar world grew, guitar shows became more popular. One of the well-known ones is Arlington. I've done plenty of business there. And I still do, if I'm low on some stock and need to resupply. Countless axes and millions of dollars have changed hands inside the convention center doors of Arlington. But sometimes the coolest deals go down outside the doors of Arlington.

Like, right outside.

═══════

Back in 1988, my friend Chris from London and I had just finished breakfast at the hotel across the street and were making our way toward the Arlington convention center. An older fellow in a beat-up Plymouth pulled into a space near us and asked us where the entrance was. We pointed in the direction of the front door.

But, instead of heading in, we milled around like dogs on the scent to see if he had anything interesting. You never know what's going to show up.

It took him forever to park and open his trunk, but finally he pulled out two electric guitar cases—a clean, brown Fender bass case and a non-descript Fender black guitar case.

Chris and I looked at each other, and I said, "Let's do odds or evens to see who gets first dibs."

Chris agreed. I lost. "Okay, which case do you want?" I said.

He laughed. "Obviously, the brown bass case."

We asked the fellow what was inside. He told us there was a Fender Precision Bass in the brown case and a Telecaster in the other. "How much?" we asked, and he told us he wanted $600 for the bass and $450 for the Tele. Chris and I looked at each other and knew we would pay for them sight unseen.

We each handed him our money. We figured no matter what was inside we probably wouldn't get burned.

Then came the unveiling. No matter how many times I see a case opened to reveal an unseen guitar, I still get a blast of adrenaline. It's kind of like that old game show *Let's Make a Deal* where you can either hold onto your cash or pay for whatever's behind the curtain that "lovely Carol Merrill" is standing in front of. The curtain opens, and . . . sometimes you win the Cadillac, and sometimes you get saddled with a hundred pounds of steer manure.

The fellow unlatched the brown bass case, revealing a 1963 Fender Precision Bass. But the body had been stripped down to the natural wood. The neck was original finish, so it wasn't a total loss. My friend

Fender 1967 Telecaster.
(Photos by Mark Agnesi)

Chris looked over to me and shrugged, as if to say, "Okay, that's a decent enough deal."

Then came my turn. Inside the generic case was a 1967 Fender Telecaster. Not just any Telecaster. I was staring at a greenish-blue Telecaster Custom with a double bound body. Unusual colors usually means its been refinished, but as I looked closely, I realized that it was a mint Telecaster Custom with its original Lake Placid blue finish! Along with its original hangtags.

You probably can guess the value and rarity of that guitar. (You'd have to guess, because I've never seen another one.)

My friend Chris shook his head. "You are unbelievable. I win the bet and you get the best deal."

I can't disagree. What would've happened if I hadn't had that second cup of coffee at breakfast and didn't come across that guy at that precise moment? What would've happened if I'd won the odds and evens?

They say it's better to be lucky than to be talented. That is true. I have been supremely lucky in guitar dealings throughout my whole life. But I am lucky, because I am passionate. It required a lot of luck, as well as a lot of "pluck," especially during those early "Wild West" years before cell phones, the Internet, and eBay.

I kept the Telecaster Custom in my personal collection for many years, and it can be seen in my first book, *Norman's Rare Guitars: 30 Years of Guitar Collecting*. But eventually, one of my customers wanted it so badly, he made me an offer I couldn't refuse. And it was quite a bit more than $450.

I started out as a musician. But ultimately my destiny lay in searching out and supplying the best instruments I could find to the best musicians and biggest stars in the business, among many other people. And I've developed personal relationships with all of them. It's been a helluva ride. I sometimes pinch myself and wonder how I got here. Well, this is how . . .

1

MIAMI
DAZE

When I was a kid, my father gave me an extraordinary bit of advice—he told me if I could sing and accompany myself on piano, I'd never starve.

Why is this extraordinary? My father, William Harris, was a practical man. And practical men don't normally tell their children that they'd never starve if they could play music. In fact, it's usually the opposite!

My father lost his whole family during the Russian Revolution and immigrated to America without a dime and not speaking a word of Eng-

Norman playing piano. (Photo by Frances Harris)

lish. A by-the-book businessman, for a long time he made a living repairing sewing machines. Then, after World War II, he went to Japan with the Marshall Plan and acquired the rights to Brother Sewing Machines for the United States. In 1958, he sold the rights back to Japan for $1.5 million, which was a lot of money in those days, and promptly retired.

This is what I've realized, after all these years—my father was forty-seven years old when my mother, Frances, had me. So, he had experienced a good amount of life before he gave me that advice. He saw that I loved music, and in his wisdom, he supported that. I'm not sure he would've seen it that way when he was a younger man.

By the time our family moved to Miami Beach from Philadelphia, via New Orleans, my father made sure I was taking three or four piano lessons a week. By the age of thirteen, I was doing steady gigs on piano and vocals around the Miami Beach and Fort Lauderdale scene. This is around 1962.

The demand for live music was very different back then. Bands were expected to play between three and six sets a night. Live bands were used for everything, from your daughter's sweet sixteen, to car dealership openings, hotel gigs, and conventions. The long-playing stereo record was only a few years old. The only DJs were cats who spun the 45s down at the local radio station. I would literally work every night, all night, and most of the time make decent money doing it. I was always playing with older guys and often had to pretend I was older than I was.

By junior high, I joined a group called the Aztecs, whose gimmick was to wear those colorful patchwork Seminole Indian jackets on stage, pretending we were real Indians. (Back then, the prevailing thought was that you had to have a gimmick to stand out. I would show you some pictures of this band, but it might prove too embarrassing.)

The Aztecs played for several years around Miami. I remember a

2

couple of stories from those days with the Aztecs. One time we saw an ad in the *Miami Herald* of a nightclub advertising for live entertainment. We answered the ad, and the club owner invited us to audition on a Friday night. It was to be a one-set audition. We arrived, set up our gear, and played the set, and the crowd was very receptive. At the end of the first set, the club owner came to us and said, "The people really like you. Why don't you finish out the night with three more sets." He assured us that he would take care of us at the end of the night. After playing those sets, we went into the club owner's office to get paid. He was sitting at his desk and reached into the top drawer. He pulled out a gun and placed it on top of his desk. He said, "Why don't you guys pack up your equipment and get out." We were underage, extremely frightened, and didn't know what to do, so we left. We later found out from our other friends who were musicians that this was commonplace at this club. The club owner was a small time mafioso, and this was his way to get free entertainment on the weekends.

Another story was from a gig at a hotel on Miami Beach. I would take a bus to the gig, and our drummer, Gerry, would have his mom drive our equipment and some of the members of the band. Remember, we were still underage. As I went backstage into the dressing room to change from my street clothes into my Seminole jacket, our guitar player, Larry, informed me that he wasn't feeling very well. Later, while we were playing, he let me know that he puked backstage. After the gig, when I went to put on my street clothes, I discovered that Larry had thrown up all over my shirt. I had to wear my Seminole Indian jacket on the bus ride home at three in the morning. There was only one other person there besides the bus driver, and he was a tough looking black dude. I sat down and he stared at me long and hard. It was really uncomfortable. Then he got up and walked toward me. "Nice jacket, man," he said, and got off.

We were lucky to play with some headliners, and one memorable gig was backing up Billy Joe Royal, a great singer who had a couple big hits with "Down in the Boondocks," and "I Knew You When." Billy Joe traveled with his musical director, a little guy called "the Tick," and they'd save money by using local musicians. Because I was the keyboard player, I was supposed to be the knowledgeable one in the band, so when the Tick played me one of his new tunes on the record, I replied, "No sweat, I got this," even though I hadn't listened to the whole record and did not know it modulated up a half step midway through the song. During the show, the Tick was playing guitar. He called the tune and moved the key up a half step, and we're all sitting there in the original key, bewildered. So, we moved it up, but then Tick moved it down, and never the twain shall meet. Suffice it to say, it was a night Billy Joe Royal never forgot!

The Aztecs played two summers as the house band up at a dude ranch type resort in Lake George, in upstate New York. We'd play four or five sets a day, six days a week, for $125 a week, including room and board, pretty good money for the time.

Our responsibilities as the house band didn't stop us from doing stupid kid stuff. It was 1968, and the drug era was kicking into "high" gear. Somehow our drummer convinced his mom to send up an air cooler that we had lined with a pound of pot. The poor, unsuspecting woman was a schoolteacher, very straight-laced, who had no idea what it contained when she shipped it. We all went to pick it up at the Albany, New York, bus station and vaguely wondered whether the DEA would be waiting for us on the tarmac. No, we didn't get popped and were elated as we rolled massive doobies on the way back to Lake George.

We used that pot all summer long. I'm not advocating this behavior but just telling the truth. If my mom were still alive, believe me, I would not be so candid about these things. Information like this might have given her a heart attack.

=====

My dad, who was a smoker, passed away that year. It affected me so deeply that even though I was only sixteen, I moved out of the house because I wanted to remember my childhood with my mom and dad together. (In reality, I just moved to another apartment in the same building, so I still had access to her top-notch cooking and laundry services.) I was making good money playing music, and I also lived on a small allowance that had been set up for me, in my dad's will.

Lake George was the plateau for the Aztecs, and I soon joined a band called the Bangles, which consisted of two very talented Micasouki Indian brothers, Lee and Steve Tiger. Being a decent singer and okay Hammond organ player with huge hair, I was a pretty hot commodity. The Bangles was the first band I was in that primarily did original material. Prior to my being in the band, Joey Spampinato from the band NRBQ was the bass player. Joey can be seen as the bass player in Keith Richards's movie, *Hail! Hail! Rock 'n' Roll*, a tribute to Chuck Berry.

Our guitar player was Frank Trabenello, who was a fine musician. However, his only claim to fame would be having his image used on a billboard all across the country saying, "Make America Beautiful, Get a Haircut." Frank had a pretty wild 'fro, and was paid $20 to let his picture be used on this billboard. He should have had me negotiate his deal.

We had a gig at a club called The World. It was a converted airplane hangar, with a stage about twenty feet up in the air. The Bangles later became one of the house bands at a converted bowling alley turned

Katmandu band. (Photo by Marlene Harris)

psychedelic rock club in Miami called The Image. The other house bands were the Blues Image (who had a monster hit with "Ride Captain Ride"), NRBQ, and a group called Fantasy. We were attempting to fuse some rhythm and blues into the pop tunes of the day—we played our original tunes along with covers like "Come See About Me" by the Supremes, or "Just a Little" by the Beau Brummels, a really good group that's been forgotten today.

When we started playing at The Image, there were a few of us local bands opening for national acts such as Cream, Hendrix, the Mothers, and the Amboy Dukes. Man, it seemed like we were in the middle of it all!

———

In 1969, I married my high school sweetheart, Marlene Kain. Later that year, I formed a band called Katmandu with the excellent singer and songwriter, Bobby Caldwell, who soon was to become famous with the song "What You Won't Do for Love." I wrote a song with Bobby called

6

"Open Your Eyes," which was covered by many people. It was recently sampled by Common and is also on John Legend's latest record. Over the years I've earned quite a few royalties off that tune, but as time goes on, the trickle of money gets less and less. Unfortunately, that's par for the course for the music business these days.

Katmandu ultimately was my play for the big time. But more importantly, my involvement with the group inadvertently got me started in the vintage instrument business. Bobby Jabo had a 1962 Gibson ES-335. Both of our guitar players switched off playing this one guitar. They both pointed out the differences to me between the old 335 and the new ones we were seeing in stores in the late sixties—the wide, flat neck, the early humbucking pickups. They convinced me that the older guitar played and sounded better than any new ones we were seeing at the time. This was my intro to vintage guitars. Bobby Caldwell and Bobby Jabo were both solid guitar players, bassists, and singers. But they didn't have a bass.

I told them, "I like bass. Why don't I buy one, and you guys can switch off playing it, and maybe I'll try to learn how to play it myself."

I saw an ad in the newspaper for a Fender Jazz Bass, and I went out to Liberty City, which was a predominantly black neighborhood. At the time, my favorite blues and R&B band in town was called Frank Williams and the Rocketeers, featuring Little Beaver on guitar. They were just the most kickass band in all of Miami, and I loved them.

So I bought this 1962 Fender Jazz Bass from this guy, and I noticed he signed the receipt "Frank Williams." I said to him, "You're not the Frank Williams of the Rocketeers," and he told me he was. I said, "Oh, man, I love all your stuff. I dig Little Beaver on guitar," and then I started naming all his tunes. He was impressed that this young, white kid was that familiar with his music. It's not like he gave me a discount or anything. There were a couple of things that resulted from that transaction. The first is that I actually bought the bass from one of my idols, my first time out! That is what can be called a "big time miracle."

Now, aficionados will talk all day long about why vintage guitars are superior. Not only are they made with better materials, and better wood and wire in their pickups, but something happens to them over the years, after they've been played a lot. They get imbued with mojo from being used and abused in all those sweaty cigarette smoke–filled rooms. It becomes a fetishistic object to musicians. This bass, as a result of a thousand nights of R&B groove, had that intangible *something*.

As soon as I brought the bass home, everyone wanted to buy it from me. It played great and it had a great sound. It had real charisma. My instincts with it had been right on. So, I started thinking, maybe I could make a few extra bucks buying up some of these old instruments and selling them. It was the Frank Williams bass that started it all for me.

You might be wondering what happened to that bass. Well, I held onto it for a number of years, refusing to sell it. Katmandu used it for all our shows and our recording sessions. We brought it to LA after we made the move west. One night, we were playing a showcase gig at Randy Ostin's house (the son of Warner Brothers' record head, Mo Ostin). When I returned from a break, I discovered that someone had stolen the bass right off the bandstand. It's ironic, because this happened in a beautiful, private house, not some sleazy club. That really hurt. I'm still looking for the damn thing!

Little Richard Penniman (yes, *the* Little Richard) ended up paying for its replacement—a refinished, white stack-knobbed Jazz Bass, which, incidentally, I still have in my collection . . . But that's another part of the story.

2

DRAFT BOARD
'69

The late sixties was a precarious time if you were a young man not in college or without a medical deferment that would keep you out of the Vietnam War. Like many of my generation, I didn't support the war and had no intention of becoming a large target, which I would have been!

I was making a solid living playing music, but I could see I'd be an easy target if I wasn't able to keep my grades up at the University of Miami and was drafted. I first went in with a major in accounting and a minor in music. After doing long and tedious accounting problems without a calculator, I realized this was never going to work, so I changed my major to filmmaking. I was looking for something a little more interesting and a lot easier.

I was burning the candle at both ends. It was not easy focusing on schoolwork, after driving to Fort Lauderdale every night, seventy miles each way, playing gigs late, then trying to get up to get to morning classes. My heart just wasn't into college—especially all those complicated formulas you had to learn when I was studying accounting. They bored me. However, the problem was, if I flunked out, it would remove another barrier between the draft board and me.

I shared my fears with my buddy Bobby Kosser, who later became a comedian. He told me I'd better start building up my case by establishing some kind of medical history, if and when I got called up.

I immediately started seeing a psychiatrist, Dr. Steven Harris (no relation), and Bobby would tell me exactly what to say to the shrink before each appointment. If the doctor asked me to draw a picture of my father, I was supposed to draw him with gigantic hands, which meant that he used to beat me. No windows in my house meant some other traumatic event, which escapes me all these years later. I told Dr. Harris that I had recurring acid flashbacks, and he prescribed Thorazine for me, which I never took. Everything I said must have been in his school "textbook," and he ate it up. I must have been one of his most classic cases. I always loved to see his reactions when I answered his questions.

A lottery was instituted in the draft and I received a number of 280 out of 365. I thought this was enough to keep me from doing military service. Two weeks later, I received a notice to report for my physical, and I was informed to bring my toothbrush only! Needless to say, this scared the crap out of me.

I had to put Bobby's full plan into action. I didn't shave or shower for a week. I stank, and I looked like an absolute maniac. I pulled out my "crazy" file from the doctor and went down to the draft board. There were about ten guys that I knew from school sitting there, all in various states of crazy. They were all pulling a similar hustle. It was hard not to break up seeing all the wacko roles these guys were playing, poorly. I was trying to keep a straight face, when my friend Kenny Gruber opened the door and screamed out at the top of his lungs, "Oh, my stomach!" I recognized his voice and almost broke up laughing. This surely would have blown my cover.

There was a fifteen-step process that everyone had to go through, and I took my time on number one. In fact, it took me about an hour just to write my name. But that wasn't all I had to do. There were about four or five black dudes around me at about step number five. I forced myself to cry in front of all of them, and they were just hooting and laughing at me, but I didn't care—I was on a mission of my own, to save my ass! It was the acting performance of my life! The draft board took me from step five to step fifteen and sent me on my way, with a 1-Y classification. This meant I was declared unfit for military service. Even in a nuclear war, forget about this guy. He's nuts! The draft board alone at this point and time, with all the crazy things people were doing, could make quite a funny movie: *Draft Board '69*.

Being free of having to go to Vietnam, school started to fall by the wayside. I focused on my music, and to some extent, the lifestyle that came with it.

Getting ahold of that Fender Jazz Bass really peaked my interest in old instruments. Remember, there was virtually no information available on this huge world of vintage guitars, so I used every resource I could. There was this old guitar repairman named John Black, who was about eighty years old and the only guy in town that I could get information from. I used to drag Marlene down to his house in Hialeah and grill him for hours. He would point out to me the nuances of old guitars—the woods used on bodies, as well as fingerboards, the differences between pickups. He even used mayonnaise to polish his guitars. He would pull out some old guitar from his back room and say, "This guitar was used by the Gold Dust Twins in 1928 on a radio show!" What a character.

Pretty soon, it got around to all the musicians in town that I was getting good axes, and I became the go-to source for many of them. However, if I found something really special, I saved it for myself. I knew that the really clean ones wouldn't just come along every day. That turned out to be the smartest thing I ever did.

I would scour the classified ads every morning. One day there was

Gibson 1949 L-5. (Photos by Jen Angkahan)

an ad that read something like "Stove, couch, refrigerator, guitar . . . "
I called up and got this elderly woman on the phone. I asked her about
the guitar, and she said it was a Gibson.

"What else do you know about it?" I said.

"Well, I can see it's got four, no six strings on it. My husband and I
are leaving town, and he instructed me to get rid of all this stuff. The
price is $25."

"Tell you what," I said. "I'll give you $20 for it, sight unseen."

So I drove over there as quickly as possible, and when she opened
the door, I saw all this junk lying around. But off to the side, leaning up
against the wall was this beautiful brown case. I hardly knew anything
about guitars, but I could tell that this case was pretty special, and I
couldn't believe that my $20 guitar was in it. I expected to see some beat
up piece of junk.

We laid the case on the floor, she opened it up, and inside it was

this beautiful, blond Gibson L-5 Premiere. Looking back, this could
have been the beginning of my obsession with blond archtops. The L-5
premiere represented the state of Gibson's art in 1939. It was a fully
carved-top guitar with the best appointments, and the *Premiere* meant
that it was a Cutaway, which was a major innovation at that time. Of
course I knew nothing about that, but I could see that this was a spectacular instrument. I paid her the $20 and immediately took it to my
buddy in Miami, Ed Oleck, who was already buying and selling old guitars. He told me what the *Premiere* designation meant on that old white
label inside the guitar, it meant the first Cutaways. He also wanted to
buy it from me, but I was not about to sell it.

In the meantime, Katmandu was firing on all cylinders. We continued having a steady gig at a nightclub called The Flying Machine in
Fort Lauderdale, whose entrance was an old seaplane, hence its name.
I was there a lot. I made friends with all the waitresses. Mind you, I was
living with my soon-to-be wife, Marlene, and I was trying to make ends
meet. I hustled things in another fashion.

I always had the gift for turning a buck. If I saw opportunity, I took
it. And in Miami, in that era, there were quite a few opportunities in
the illegal marijuana trade. Through my Cuban buddies, I would buy
one pound of pot, then break it up into sixteen "lids," and give it to the
waitresses in the club to sell. It was an easy way to make money, and I
did quite well with it. Being a good capitalist, I reinvested my profits in
more pot.

One night, I was driving home from The Flying Machine in the pour-
ing rain at three in the morning, and I crashed my car into a telephone
pole on the 836 expressway overpass. In my trunk I had three ounces
of pot and about ten LSD trips. I immediately ran to my trunk and threw
the dope over the side of the expressway on a greenbelt. I was sleep
deprived and pretty messed up. A Good Samaritan spotted me, and my

messed-up car, and helped me get it back on the road. It was barely running, but I hoped it would get me home. The next day, Marlene and I went back to The Flying Machine in her car with my beautiful L-5 Premier in the trunk. I wanted to show the guitar to my bandmates and friends at the club. I figured I would also stop along the expressway and retrieve my dope. I spotted where my car had crashed, looked over to the side of the greenbelt, and sure enough there was my dope. I grabbed it and put it in my trunk, along with the Gibson L-5.

On the way back home to Perrine that night, we ran into some traffic, and all I can remember was a car screeching behind me. Next thing I knew— bang!—I was rear-ended! Once again, I ran to the trunk and threw the dope off to the side of the expressway. By the time the police came, I had opened the case to my L-5 and noticed a big crack in the guitar. I was in two accidents within twenty-four hours. This made me never want to get into a car again, but of course I had no choice.

Marlene and I went to the emergency room because we experienced whiplash. After being treated, we went back to my apartment. My bandmates met me there, and I ran down the whole story to them, including my L-5 getting damaged and me throwing my dope off to the side of the expressway once again. Of course my bandmates encouraged me to go back for the dope once again. We got in the car and went back to the spot of the accident, stopped on the expressway, and I jumped out to once again retrieve my dope. A police car spotted us and made me pull over. He said, "What are you crazy? Why are you stopping on the expressway?" Fortunately, I was thinking quickly, and said, "I thought I heard something fall off my car, possibly my bumper." The cop actually believed my story and told me to get back on the expressway and go home. It was a very close call. I guess that contraband was never meant to be mine.

We reported the accident to Marlene's insurance company, and it turned out that my friend Ed Oleck became an advisor to the insurance adjuster. He told them that they better give me $1,200 because the guitar was irreplaceable. That may not sound like a lot, but in 1969 that was some serious money. And I used it to invest in my new business buying and selling guitars.

———————

Meanwhile, I had reinvested a lot of my profits from selling pot into more stash, and I had accumulated about twenty pounds, which I had stashed in my luminous ceiling in my kitchen. One of the Cuban guys that I was buying my pot from told me that we had to check out this new movie called *Joe*, with Peter Boyle. (If you like the actress Susan Sarandon, I suggest you see this film, immediately.) So, one night, I took Marlene out on a date to see the movie, and when we returned, the first thing I saw was that the lock on the door had been broken. Sure enough, all my pot was gone, obviously an inside job orchestrated by my Cuban "friend."

I was completely wiped out. I couldn't even call the police and tell them I'd been robbed. Understandably, this was the end of my career as a pot dealer. It was quite a harsh learning experience, but at least I realized that business can be a lot less volatile if it's conducted on the right side of the law. I did not want to be a big time dealer or do business with those unsavory characters. I was just young and dumb. But right then and there, I decided I'd only deal in legitimate products in the future, which, of course, eventually became guitars. I often think if the police had nailed me for that amount of dope in 1969, I'd probably still be serving time today, so in a sense it was really lucky that I got ripped off and not busted!

Music was still my overriding passion. All other pursuits took a backseat to it. Katmandu was getting really popular, and we even opened up for the Allman Brothers on a field in front of the Miami Beach auditorium in 1970. Whenever I tell people that, the first thing they want to know is if Duane Allman blew my mind at that gig. Honestly, he didn't have that much impact on me that day. We all knew they were a good band. But probably as a result of the fact that it was outdoors, and that they were using a primitive PA system, it just didn't seem that heavy.

As a result of that gig, we got a record deal. The label was called Mainstream Records, and their big seller was Big Brother and the Holding Company with Janis Joplin. So we figured we'd finally made it. The owner, Bob Shad, was a pretty well known jazz producer, who had recorded Charlie Parker and Clifford Brown and was now trying to jump on the rock-and-roll bandwagon.

We went into the legendary Criteria Studios to record at the same time that Derek and the Dominoes were recording the Layla album. With one big difference—Clapton and crew recorded that album over a period of months, whereas we recorded ours in twenty-four hours and, unfortunately, it sounded like it! We were really too green to be churning out a record at that pace, but Shad was desperate for material. The session was shit.

To make matters worse, we found out shortly after signing that Big Brother was suing the label, because they were getting screwed on their royalties. Needless to say, we didn't get much promotion and the label was already in trouble.

But it all wasn't a complete wash. When we were recording at Criteria, Little Richard and his brother, Peyton Penniman, heard us and took an interest in our future. Richard told me that I was one of the "best white singers" he'd ever heard and, of course, I ate that up.

Though Richard was about a decade removed from the peak of his career, he was still a bankable and working act. He told us that we'd never make it in Miami and that we'd have to move to LA, and he could set us up with Mo Ostin at Warner Brothers records.

That was all the encouragement we needed. We packed up every-thing and prepared to drive across country. I did leave some stuff in Miami, in case I'd want to move back. But, as it happens with so many things in life, I never did go back to Miami to live.

I, like many, wanted to take my shot at the music business.

3

MOVING TO CALIFORNIA

The thriving, creative music scene in Miami, which had nurtured so many bands, practically evaporated overnight.

When the Blues Image, who everyone agreed was the best band in the state, split for Los Angeles, that was the first shot across the bow. Soon, NRBQ moved back up to New York state. Mike Pinera, the monster guitar player from the Blues Image, urged us to go west, so it seemed like a no-brainer. Miami rock and roll was never the same after that.

It was 1970. Making our play for the "big time," I was also about to get a dose of "big-time" reality.

It turned out Little Richard, in spite of his iconic status, was on the Musician's Union's "Do Not Perform For" list. Apparently he had stiffed some former members of his band, and they had filed a grievance against him.

Before we even arrived in LA, Richard had us stop over for one of his gigs opposite B.B. King in a beautiful venue in Lake Tahoe called The King's Castle. Then brand new, it was one of the first Arthurian-themed casinos in the world, though now it's a Hyatt Regency.

Richard and his musical director, Bobby Forte (veteran R&B tenor sax player with Ray Charles and Bobby Blue Bland, among others) had a fifteen-piece band waiting for him there. Well, the first night was such a disaster that Richard had us come up to back him up! He figured all these jazz players had to know Little Richard tunes, but those cats had been too busy studying Bird or getting too high to give a shit.

Richard's producer Bumps Blackwell drove them hard the next few days, and the week-long stand went pretty smoothly from then on.

Forte, though a great player, was a junkie, like so many horn players back in the day. His tenor was held together by rubber bands through most of the gigs. On the last night, he stepped up to the mike for his solo, empty-handed. He had pawned his horn for dope and was so high that he didn't know the difference! Richard bawled him out on the bandstand, and it was embarrassing all around. Though it was kind of funny at the time, it showed how tough life could be for some of these cats.

When we landed in LA, we all took up residence at Richard's "office," the Carolina Pines Motel, on La Brea and Sunset, in Hollywood. It was a fifties modern motel based around a pool, which was already starting to get funky by the seventies. (It's now the site of a Comfort Inn.) Richard and his entourage had about seven or eight rooms there. It was right next door to a Copper Penny coffee shop, one of the only places in Hollywood that served grits with breakfast.

Richard had an open account with the motel, but even then I was able to see the transient nature of his living—a day-to-day existence. But because we were newbies in town, we had no place else to go, so we stuck around for a while.

You gotta have wheels in LA, so Richard set us up in a house on Raynetta Drive in Sherman Oaks, along with a 1961 Chevy station wagon that looked like it had barely survived the demolition derby. This car was a total eyesore and ran every other Thursday. Because no one in the house got up before noon, I had the beater to myself every morning to search out instruments. One day its brakes died, so we just abandoned it out on Sunset Boulevard.

We eventually ended up with a van, which we used to drive to all our gigs. Many times we got in the van, rolled up a fatty, and got completely lost in LA. If you don't know the freeway system, it can be quite treacherous. Being slightly hampered didn't help matters any. There were no navigation systems at that time.

I remember playing in a club in Venice Beach that was right adjacent to Synanon (the famous cult and drug rehabilitation center, which is now a hotel). One night we finished our set and were loading up our gear, when an old lady came out wearing just a blanket and one stocking. I felt bad for her, so I gave her a few dollars. I don't know if she thought I was propositioning her, but she took off the blanket and began chasing me around the van. Stark-raving naked! All I can say is this was quite an area of town. LA rocked! What a time to be in Los Angeles.

Even though we hardly had any gigs, we knew that we needed to rehearse, so the house in Sherman Oaks came in handy for that. You can just imagine what was going on there, with a group of eighteen to twenty year olds. The house didn't have a stick of furniture, except for waterbeds (which were everywhere in 1970). We would eat dinner out of tin pans that we purchased at the Eagle Army Navy store. There was no air-conditioning, so on hot days, we'd cool off in the frozen food section at the local grocery store.

Guests used to come and go at all hours of the day and night. One of them was my Cuban buddy from Miami named Lache, who showed up with a load of cocaine. On a lark, he'd bought a Corvette from another guy's girlfriend, who happened to be a junkie. One night, Marlene and I, and some of my bandmates, came back to the house after a fun-filled day at Disneyland, when we were accosted by some scary looking black dudes. They shoved us inside and pulled out a machete, demanding that we give them the Vette. (By the way, this wouldn't be the last machete I encountered in LA.) The main guy, a menacing hulk who they called "Grease," had been hired by the girl who was the previous owner to retrieve the vehicle. After some fast and fancy talking, we finally convinced them that Lache had sold the car himself and that we didn't know where he was. A week later, we saw "Grease" at the Westward Ho Market (now Whole Foods), and we called out to him, "Hey, Grease!" He pretended he had no idea who we were and, apparently "Grease" wasn't his real name.

Needless to say, we weren't too focused on the job at hand, which was getting our music together. Richard's own career trajectory and reputation didn't help, either. But something else was gnawing at me, too. Call it self-awareness . . .

4

THE HENDRIX
OF THE ELECTRIC BASS

When you're young, you feel bulletproof. You often think that you're the "stuff," and that nothing will stand in the way of your goal. Even though I was in my early twenties back then, after spending some time in LA, I could see that there were many obstacles in the way of making it in the music business. Sometimes they had to do with talent, and sometimes they had to do with luck. You needed at least a bit of both to get any traction. Along those lines, I often thought about a

Norman and Jaco Pastorius, early '70s, at Monty's Restaurant. (Photo by Marlene Harris)

musician who had a big impact on me back in Fort Lauderdale, a couple of years before I made the move to LA.

We had been auditioning to play in a club called The She in Fort Lauderdale, which was owned by the same people who owned The Flying Machine. After playing a couple of tunes, we stepped outside to smoke a joint, and suddenly I heard some guy just ripping it to shreds on my Hammond B3. I walked inside, and there was this clean-cut, young seventeen-year-old kid just killing it, sounding like Jimmy Smith.

"Man, you sound great," I told him.

The kid shrugged it off. "Well, I'm really a bass player."

"Well, what the hell does that make me?" I asked, half-jokingly.

That was my introduction to the great Jaco Pastorius. After that, we became really close friends. My band, Katmandu, was pretty popular, and we'd often have Jaco's band, Woodchuck, open for us. Woodchuck was a trio comprised of bass, drums, and Hammond B3, with the drummer, Bob Hertzog, doing all the singing. It was a crude set-up, but these clean-cut nerdy kids were just funkier than hell. They would do covers of "Peak of Love" by Bobby McClure, or "Ninety-Nine and a Half" by Wilson Pickett, and start the tune real straight, but by the third verse they'd be out there in the ozone, like Sun Ra.

The public really didn't understand them, but every hip musician in town would come to check out what Jaco was doing. He just blew everybody else away. So much so, that a fine local bass player, Bob Bobbing, used to follow him around with a Wollensak tape recorder and record all his gigs, much like this cat Dean Benedetti did with Charlie Parker. Thank God he did, for these killer cuts all made it into the excellent *Jaco: The Early Years* CD.

Jaco was a modest, straitlaced-looking innocent, compared with us long-haired wild men. Drug and alcohol free. In other words, very different from what his image was to become, years later.

He once said to me, "You guys will probably do well. You guys play good. You got the whole look down and everything."

But the truth was, Jaco and his trio just buried us. I knew it in my heart. But I also knew there was a big possibility that Jaco would just languish in the Miami scene. It was a crapshoot. The general audiences, not understanding Jaco, showed how arbitrary the music business was. Even if you were the best, it didn't necessarily mean shit.

Back in Miami, I had a refinished dot neck Jazz Bass that Jaco desperately wanted. I ended up trading it to him for a fairly clean four-by-ten Bassman amp. (This bass is all over the *Jaco, the Early Years* booklet.) Jaco later sold that bass to a Miami musician and friend of mine, John Paulus, who later came out to play in one of my LA bands in the early seventies, the Angel City Rhythm Band.

Paulus later played with John Mayall for many years. After owning the bass for quite a few years, Paulus figured it was time to part with it. Because I had been one of its first owners and knew all about its history, he asked me to help him sell it. With that history, we easily sold it to a collector in Japan, where it resides still. An authentic Jaco bass—an amazing and iconic piece of music memorabilia.

———

Mike Pinera was another case in point. As the driving creative force in the Blues Image, he was at the top of the list of the heaviest guitar players in town. Whenever Hendrix or Cream came to Miami, he was the one they wanted to jam with. When the Blues Image knocked it out of the park with "Ride Captain Ride" (still one of the catchiest songs of the era), there was no doubt in anybody's mind that the group would go right to the top. They were that good. Instead, the record label induced Mike to join the Iron Butterfly with a big signing bonus. The Blues Image, even with Mike Pinera, one of the best groups I'd ever heard, became a proverbial one-hit wonder, and the Iron Butterfly continued their descent into metal obscurity. One wrong move and all that promise, down the drain.

So in hindsight, all those older instruments I was buying, selling, and stashing away were my security blanket. I brought about fifty or sixty with me to LA in 1970. The demand for them was consistent, while the success or failure of a group was unpredictable.

5

UNION DUES, MUSIC STORES, AND BUYING STRATEGY

I was discovering quickly that Los Angeles was a huge metropolis, which had its pluses and its minuses.

A minus was the fact that Katmandu, after being a well-loved non-stop-gigging band in Miami, was scuffling in LA. We had to start all over, and it wasn't going good.

A plus was the flip side of that—people from all over the country also came to LA to make it big and when things didn't work out, they'd often have to sell their instruments to get home. So at least one of my careers was growing nicely. I was also psyched this was the home of Fender guitars and Rickenbacker guitars, and I might be able get my hands on stuff "closer to the source."

The *LA Times* was my most important resource. Part of my detective work consisted of following the newspaper trucks as they left the printers and determining where their first stop was to drop off the papers. I soon found out that the Sunday paper came out Saturday morning at 5:00 a.m., and the first stop was the Greyhound bus station off Main Street in downtown LA. This was Saturday's news with the Sunday classified section.

At 5:00 a.m., it was fairly dangerous down there, chock-full of homeless and desperate people. I saw fights and loads of drugged-out people and many things that might deter other people. I was kind of like a Rain

Man when it came to guitars. I had the full-on fever of something that later became known as GAS (Guitar Acquisition Syndrome). That's all I was interested in, and I was a pit bull at it.

Sometimes an ad would be very vague like "Gibson guitar" or "Fender guitar" and "amp." I knew enough about the models to ask the proper questions, to determine if it was worth schlepping out to West Covina or Pomona to see it. If there wasn't some type of label inside the guitar or a decal, I would ask questions on the phone such as, "Where it says Gibson on the headstock, is that a gold decal or is it in Mother of Pearl?" Anything upscale would have Gibson in pearl and possibly some other design underneath it. As far as guitars with gold decals go, I would first have to determine if it was hollow, if it had *f*-holes or a center hole. If it was a solid body, I would have to ask the color and how many points or cutaways the guitar had, as well as how many volume and tone knobs it had. If it was solid and a sunburst, it would generally be a Les Paul Jr. or Melody Maker. If it was hollow, I would have to determine if it had *f*-holes or a round hole. If it was flat-top, it could be anything from an LG-0 to a B-25, or if it was a larger body, it was probably a J-45 or J-50.

At one point there was a guy who was on to what I was doing. Somehow he must have been following me and figured out my strategy. I was down at the Greyhound bus station on a Saturday morning to get the *LA Times,* and I saw an ad for a Fender Precision Bass and Bassman amplifier. I drilled the seller to get whatever information I could and determined that it was a 1952 Precision Bass, and an early-1950s tweed Fender Bassman amp with one 15-inch speaker. He was asking $1,000 for both and claimed to be the original owner. He was out in Simi Valley, about a forty-five-minute drive from where I was. A deal like this always got me very excited. I got into the Chevy beater and jumped on the 405 freeway heading toward Simi Valley, going about seventy-five miles per hour. I looked over to my right and saw this other car almost in a dead heat with me. I recognized the driver and realized that he was heading to buy the same guitar.

We both raced to Simi Valley, got off the freeway, and we were going so fast, we both passed the street we needed to turn on to. We both doubled back to the house, and I knew I was going to have to make a move. In those days, I used to carry quite a bit of cash, just in case I found anything. When we both got out of the car, I told the other guy that the seller was asking $1,000 for both the guitar and amp. I said if we get into a bidding war, the only person that's going to win is the seller, and I was determined to outbid this other buyer.

I pulled out a big wad of cash and got right up into his face. "I'm going to buy both of these for $1,000 and I'm going to give you the amp for nothing, but if I ever see you again doing this, I will outbid you and you'll go home with nothing, even if I lose money!" I was protecting my turf, and it must've worked. I never saw this other buyer again. I hated to strong-arm him, but my livelihood was at stake. I ended up with a beautiful bass, he ended up with a beautiful amp, and that was the last I've ever seen of him.

=======

My band Katmandu was sporadically working, mainly because we played original material, and that made it difficult to get regular club gigs. Most club owners wanted us to play the Top 40 hits of the day, and it felt like a compromise. However, this very issue started to drive a wedge between us all.

When we all first got together, Bobby Caldwell was more of a Jeff Beck, rock 'n' roll type guitar player. I was more into R&B and that influenced the band quite a bit. I sang the lead on 90 percent of the tunes we did. But when we finally recorded in LA, I encountered somewhat of a rude awakening. Bobby's voice had a certain quality that translated to tape very easily. My voice kind of smothered the tracks but his had a transparency that recorded very nicely. It kind of upset me, because I was the singer of the band. But in retrospect, it of course helped drive me more in the direction of the vintage instrument business.

Eventually Bobby decided to move back to Florida. He ended up signed with TK Records (who had the monster sellers, KC and the Sunshine Band) and has had quite a bit of success as both a musician and songwriter. Remaining in California, I figured I could hook up with some of the other quality musicians I had met through my guitar business and maybe buy some time until my musical career might start to happen.

Every morning, being situated in a very central location, I would get in my car and drive in one direction or another. One day I might go south into Santa Monica and work my way down through Long Beach and all the other towns between San Diego and my apartment in Sherman Oaks. Other mornings I might head east through Hollywood and eventually find my way as far as Palm Springs.

I left no stone unturned. I discovered every music store, pawnshop, thrift store, bulletin board, et cetera. I was determined to uncover any and all buried treasure out there. One of my regular stops was at the Hollywood Musician's Union, Local 47, on Vine Street. I can't even tell you how many instruments I found from listings on the bulletin board in there. The membership handbook also became useful, as I cold-called many musicians. This was long before cell phones, so making phone calls by the hundreds could become quite expensive, and many were toll calls.

My wife, Marlene, always very creative, suggested looking for names that sounded like older folks. I mean, how many "Delmers" "Calvins" and "Vernons" would be gigging in rock bands in the seventies? Many of these players had great older guitars and were ready to sell, to fund their retirement.

I also called players who were listed as banjo, mandolin, ukulele, or bass players. Anything with frets. I would always have the seller tell me their asking price. I would never offer pennies on the dollar, and if their asking price was reasonable, I acquired their guitars. Many times these players had large collections, as they had been endorsees of Gibson, Martin, Fender, Gretsch, Rickenbacker, D'Angelico, Stromberg, Mosrite, et cetera. I found many historical instruments by using this strategy, and I believe if I didn't do this, I never would have accumulated the number of quality instruments that have become my personal collection.

When our band was on the road, the first thing I'd do was check in with the local musician's union and get the roster, so I could start calling. My ploy was that I was a musician thinking of moving to whatever town I was in and wanted to talk to some of the locals, to see how it was going. My true motive was to call guitarists and see if they had anything to sell.

There was, of course, always a learning curve with all of this. If I called somebody early in the day, and they had a guitar I was interested in, it gave them a chance to call music stores to get a value, or find someone else to bid against me. So I started making the calls after 6:00 p.m., so they couldn't get ahold of anybody. This is long before someone could just look up the value of a guitar on the Internet or even in a book.

I also used to put ads in all the local newspapers, including the *Daily News*, and the now-defunct *Herald Examiner*. I was always playing around with the wording for newspaper ads so that they might attract attention. Marlene came up with a suggestion to put some of my guitar-wanted ads in the newspaper section under "Horses for Sale." Her logic was that cowboys often played guitar. Oddly enough, I ended up finding some of the coolest guitars that way, including an incredible prewar

Martin 000-42, several prewar D-18s and even a few 1950s electric Gibsons and Fenders along the way.

========

I made it my job to visit all the local music stores listed in the Yellow Pages. I did quite a lot of business with Sol Betnun's Music Store on Larchmont Street in Hollywood. It was actually a ramshackle house, chock-full of various kinds of equipment. Guitars and amps were stuffed high to the rafters, and you'd have to dig around not to miss anything.

Sol was an older gentleman, a professional union horn player from a bygone time, who opened his store in the sixties when he saw the writing on the wall for jazz and swing. Though he had no love for the new music, clearly Sol saw great opportunity in dealing in all those kids' obsessions with guitars who were being spawned by the Beatles' popularity.

I liked Sol because he was willing to make deals. He had a nice selection of used instruments and loved to trade with me, as long as I kicked some cash into the equation. There was always a huge influx of new acquisitions coming in, and I was there trying to make deals on anything I felt was a good investment.

The scene in his store was always crazy. His family was, to put it mildly, extremely colorful. Sol would come into the store and was always wearing about two shirts, three sweaters, and an overcoat, even though this was LA, and it was probably eighty degrees outside. His wife, Lil, was also a character, and they had this little Chihuahua that acted like it owned the place.

My friend Chris Bristol, who later became a big shot at the Roland Corporation, basically ran the store. Chris had a great understanding of quality guitars and was always easy to deal with. When Sol wouldn't be moved, Chris would step in to smooth the deal, understanding that it would have to make sense for both of us.

In Pasadena, my old friend Bob Page also ran a store called The Guitar Shoppe. Bob's specialty at the time was acoustic instruments. It was kind of in the basement of this shopping center in downtown Pasadena. He had at one time played with the iconic sixties band the Association, which had monster hits with "Along came Mary," "Never My Love," "Cherish," and quite a few others, so he had some experience with "the big time." I believe he joined the band for a while but ended up opening his store in Pasadena.

Bob was very knowledgeable about older guitars, and I learned a lot from him. This may be difficult to believe these days, but there was no published information available on anything! You had to seek out people who had experience with old guitars and wheedle them for their insights. I was relentless on that front. I had an insatiable desire to find out all I could.

I believe the first Martin Herringbone D-28 that I ever owned came from Bob. Over time, I purchased a treasure trove of instruments from him. We traded on a regular basis, and I used to stop by Bob's place at least once a week. My friend Dave DiMartino, who was one of the early founding fathers of Guitar Center, got his start with Bob.

There was a store in the Redondo Beach area that I did some business with called Hogan's House of Music. When I headed south each week in my car, I always made sure I dropped in there. Later on I found out that one of the guys that I was dealing with at Hogan's, Ron Block, an excellent guitar player, joined Allison Krauss and Union Station and is still having great success in the music business.

There were other "establishment" places in Hollywood, like the famous Wallich's Music City on Sunset and Vine, which had been an institution in LA, back since the music business was based around selling

Martin 1941 Herringbone D-28. (Photos by Jen Angkahan)

sheet music. Glen Wallich had been one of the founding partners of Capitol Records with Johnny Mercer in the forties. Even in the seventies, Wallich's was still selling sheet music, but I didn't really deal with them much. I was the youngster coming in with my wild "jew-fro," a renegade willing to pay crazy high prices for used guitars. I believe they thought I was crazy. The guitars I was buying were later referred to as vintage, and they're still around while, sadly, Wallichs has been long gone for decades.

—

Probably the best places to find stuff back then were the pawnshops. They were a very valuable resource. The owners would also inadvertently divulge crucial information by letting me inspect all the instruments that came into their stores. Sometimes even before they came out of pawn.

On Van Nuys Boulevard in the San Fernando Valley, there was a pocket of about five or six pawnshops within a two-block area. There was a shop called San Fernando Jewelry and Loan, owned by my friend Mark Zimmelman's family. Mark was a good guitar player who went to Berklee School of Music and later became a famous diamond broker.

One of the most colorful areas was downtown Los Angeles. The pawnshops were almost all on Main Street. This area was a little more sketchy, but I acquired lots of great stuff there. There was one called Eagle Loan and Jewelry, where I did a lot of business. The older fellow who ran the place really took a liking to me and sold me some unbelievable instruments, including early Les Pauls, Strats, Teles, and high-end Martins. In those days, you could actually get those kinds of guitars from pawnshops!

One of the wildest of those places was Mad Man Louie's Pawnshop. I found lots of cool stuff in his pawnshop. Old Les Pauls and all of the models anyone might ever want would regularly appear in the window.

I guess you had to have a gimmick to stand out from the crowd, and Louie pretended he was crazy. He was quite old, and his son basically ran the place. They always had this funny shtick, riffing off each other.

I would come in, find some guitars that I wanted, and negotiate the deal with Louie. After the deal was made, his son would take his shoe off and start banging it on the counter. He would always say to his dad, "What are you crazy? You can't sell that guitar for that little!" That routine happened almost every time I bought a guitar from them. It was always hilarious. I never knew if they were kidding or if they were serious.

I don't know if any of this shit means anything to anyone else, but when you're a young man, it makes an impression. It's important to have fun and laugh, in whatever your business is. I wouldn't trade these memories for anything.

Eventually, the local stores came to know me as sort of a renegade guitar buyer and seller. Most of them were not that interested in buying used guitars, so I became an outlet for them to sell their trade-ins. They probably thought I was crazy for paying more for used guitars than new guitars. But eventually it became more than evident that I had amassed a decent collection of collectable instruments and customers started coming to me, via word of mouth.

One such store was University Music in West LA on Wilshire Boulevard. The owner, Dale Rossman, liked my band, and he and I became good friends. Little did I know that he would send a customer to me that would change the course of my guitar-selling life.

6

ENCOUNTER WITH
A BEATLE

E arly one morning in 1973, I received a call from Dale Rossman saying that he had an important customer whose Les Paul had been stolen and he was looking to replace it. When I pressed him, he just told me to "get your ass over here, but quick!" When I protested, he said, "Don't let me down, Norm. I told George Harrison that you'd deliver . . . "

George Harrison? I never had known Dale to lie to me, but I had a very hard time believing that a real Beatle was in Dale's store and that I was about to meet him. Growing up at the time, you have to understand that the Beatles were bigger than life itself. If you combined Prince, Beyonce, the president, and tossed in a smattering of Nelson Mandela, it still wouldn't compare to meeting a real Beatle!

I anxiously raced over to University Music. When I got there, no one was in the store but Dale, all by himself. I thought to myself, great, a practical joke.

I asked, "So where the hell is George Harrison?"

"Next door getting a slice of pizza," he said, nonchalantly. With that, the front door opened and George Harrison and Mal Evans (the Beatles' road manager) entered. I was pretty much in complete shock. I kept looking at George and kept thinking, this has got to be a double. It could not really be George Harrison! But, in fact, it was. His album, *Liv-*

Norman and George Harrison. (Photo by Marlene Harris)

ing in the Material World, had just been released, and his single "Give Me Love" was racing up the charts.

We began talking. His beloved red 1950s Les Paul Standard (nicknamed "Lucy" for Lucille Ball, also a redhead) that had been given to him by Eric Clapton, had been stolen. The guitar had become legend as the one played by Clapton on the "While My Guitar Gently Weeps" solo and had been prominently featured in the Beatles "Revolution" video. There was a lot of lore surrounding the guitar, and the instrument meant a lot to George. In fact, we now know that the Paul started life as a 1957 Goldtop, was bought by John Sebastian of the Lovin' Spoonful, then sold to Rick Derringer of the McCoys, who refinished it red, then sold it to a music store that sold it to Clapton.

The thief had sold the guitar to Whalin's Sound City Music in Hollywood, who had in turn flipped it to a musician who lived part of the time in California and the rest of the time in Mexico. George Whalin had the information on the buyer, and Harrison got in touch with him, asking if he would please sell it back to him.

The buyer replied that he would be happy to see the guitar back with George, but he felt he purchased the guitar in good faith and would want an equivalent replacement for the guitar. Another late-1950s Gibson Les Paul Standard! George was given my friend Dale's number and was told that Dale could possibly find a replacement.

At the time I had three Sunburst Les Paul Standards from the time period. Dale knew this, and that's why he called me. When I met George and Mal, I told them that the guitars were at my apartment in Sherman Oaks, and we would have to go back to my place for him to view the instruments.

George, Mal, and I got in my car and headed over to my modest apartment in Sherman Oaks. I kept looking at George because I could hardly believe that a Beatle was sitting next to me. I think George was a little paranoid that I might try to kidnap him. After a few minutes, and a joint or two later, we all relaxed a bit. Mal was a big man, and I believe that made George feel more comfortable in a stranger's presence.

We pulled into the underground parking lot at my apartment building and began walking up the stairs through the courtyard to my apartment. On the way up, a couple of my neighbors spotted George with me and I could see their shock. I opened the door and there was Marlene cleaning the apartment in her bathrobe. I told her that George Harrison was coming in, and the look on her face told me she thought I was full of crap.

Two seconds later George and Mal entered my humble abode and Marlene's jaw almost hit the floor. She made coffee while George, Mal, and I began opening guitar cases. George found a nice 1959 Gibson Les Paul flame top that he thought would be suitable to trade for Lucy. He also spotted a gorgeous 1960 flame top with a thin neck that he fell in love with and wanted to buy for himself. I told him that I wanted $1,500 (a whopping $8,200 today) each for the Les Pauls. George negotiated with me and said he loved a gorgeous 1956 Fender Stratocaster that I had, and asked me if he could buy that guitar for $750. I was so blown away to be dealing with George Harrison I said "sure," even though he was the one customer who could afford to pay ten times as much. George was a tough negotiator, and he cajoled me into throwing in a tweed 1950s Princeton amp.

Even at the time I felt the prices were low, but I couldn't believe I was actually selling to George. The musician in me wanted him to have the instruments because I felt that great music would be made on them. We agreed on the deal, but no money was exchanged yet. George would have to contact the musician that had his old Les Paul and see if this deal would be acceptable.

George invited me to his house in Hollywood Hills and we spent about three days together until the deal was finally culminated. Ravi Shankar and his band were also staying at the house. I really enjoyed my time with George and Mal, and we all had a lot fun exchanging guitar and music stories.

At one point, George asked if I would be interested in trading for his Gretsch Country Gentleman. He said he was no longer playing Gretsch guitars and would trade me for some other guitar that I had. George was the first big star I ever dealt with, and I felt that nobody would believe that I actually had George's Country Gentleman. What a huge mistake!

Why didn't I do it? Well, I just thought that everyone would call me a liar. How could I possibly have George Harrison's guitar? That was before anybody even thought about memorabilia and authentication. (Although I should've!)

Apparently I wasn't thinking too clearly, but in fairness, you have to remember the context. Nobody was really looking back at the early Beatles stuff so much, especially George. There was no 1960s nostalgia then. A Gretsch by itself had limited appeal. I guess I could only blame myself for my limited perspective of history.

Of all the ones that got away, this was the biggest.

These days the prices of most of these instruments have become astronomical. Some late 1950s flame tops have sold for as much as a half-million dollars. Yet it would be next to impossible to put a numerical figure on the actual guitar that played all those licks that are permanently emblazoned in our heads from those early Beatles' albums! Such is life. I have no regrets, and the experience will be with me for as long as I live.

Ultimately, the "Lucy" guitar was returned to George, which made him very happy. He held onto her until his death and always claimed that Lucy had been kidnapped. If that's true, then I helped in paying the ransom.

As a side note, about a year ago, a lady stopped by my store telling me she remembered me from living in the apartment in Sherman Oaks. She remembered all the fuss at the apartment building the day George Harrison came by. When George, Mal, and I left my apartment that day, there was quite a crowd of people standing outside. The lady said that she, her mom, and her sister lived in that apartment building. Her sister and she were just small girls. Her mom was friendly with Marlene. She said, "I don't know if you are aware, but my sister is Paula Abdul."

In Los Angeles, you just never know who might be living next to you.

7

A GENTLEMAN
NAMED ROBBIE

My experience with George Harrison helped keep my own creative fires burning. I was so inspired by him, I continued to pursue my own music. Proximity to that much success surely had to count for something!

I joined a band called the Charlie Dawg Band that just happened to be named after lead guitarist Dan Walsh's Samoyed. Dan and the rest of the band were from Sacramento. There was Ed Robles (later known as Gabriel Black) on saxophone and vocals, Fred Gerrard on second guitar, Bud Harpham on bass, Brian Clark on drums, and me on Hammond B-3 organ. Bud Harpham eventually left the band and was replaced by Ron Blair. Ron at a later date joined a little band called Tom Petty and the Heartbreakers.

By this time, I had moved to Reseda and had opened my first store, five hundred feet of raw space at 6753 Tampa Avenue. The rent was about $480 a month. I was trying to come up with nifty names for the store, like Guitar City, or Guitar Heaven, but Marlene convinced me to use my own name for the store. Everybody just knew me as Norm, so I wanted to retain my clientele. At first I was uncomfortable calling the store Norman's Rare Guitars. Thank God I did, because the store's name and brand have remained after all these years.

A friend of mine, Scott Borden, used to consign some of my instru-

Norman's first store at 6753 Tampa Avenue, Reseda, California.
(Photo by Marlene Harris)

ments at the Whole Earth Market, which was kind of a seventies-style shopping arcade with a lot of hippy-era stuff for sale. People were selling small pyramids and telling folks if they put their cigarettes or anything inside the pyramid, it would improve in quality. This was a little nutty, but some people went for it. I needed Scott, because someone had to mind the store while I was out digging up old instruments. He was crucial to my operations but later staked out his own claim as an owner of two recording studios.

But selling was still Plan B for me. I was again burning candles at both ends—getting up at 6:00 a.m. to hunt down old guitars in the newspapers, opening the shop from 11:00 a.m. to 6:00 p.m., going out to play the clubs from 9:00 p.m. to 2:00 a.m., crashing, then starting all over again. I was still in my twenties, so I could handle the sleep deprivation.

Charlie Dawg got some good traction in the area. We toured up and down California. We played all the top clubs, including the Whiskey a

Go Go in Hollywood, and were also the house band at the infamous Topanga Corral, which inspired Jim Morrison's "Roadhouse Blues."

The Corral was the hippy hub of the hippiest canyon in LA. Canned
Heat did an album in the sixties called, *Live at the Topanga Corral*,
which had actually been recorded in Hollywood. There were a slew of
colorful characters who hung out there. "Jeff the Chef" once drove his
Harley onto the dance floor completely naked, while tripping. "Topanga
Dick" was an old beatnik who lived in this abandoned school bus behind the Corral. Often during our last set, we'd encourage Dick to come
up and recite stream-of-consciousness poetry while we grinded a slow
blues in the background.

We always liked to play funky dance music, and one night Dick was
dancing while holding this box. He would dance, then shake the box,
dance, then shake it some more. Every set he came out with this box,
held it over his head, and shook it. Finally we asked him, "What's in the
box, Dick?"

"Oh, that's Jeff. He was killed in a motorcycle accident. We're going
to spray his ashes all over the canyon. We wanted him to have a last
night dancing at the Corral."

When I look back I see how crazy it was, but we were young, and
we dug it.

In spite of the antics, the Charlie Dawg Band was really solid musically, and we performed good original material. We recorded at the
legendary Sound City Studios at the same time Lindsey Buckingham
and Stevie Nicks were working together, pre–Fleetwood Mac. The
great band War and Rick Springfield were also recording there when
we were there.

After we made a name for ourselves in LA, we got a gig playing the
state fair in Sacramento and also got booked into the famous Crabshaw
Corners (the top club in Sacramento). It was an important homecom-

Norman with Robbie Robertson at Robbie's house in Malibu. (Photo by Marlene Harris)

ing gig for the guys in the band. Everybody's friends and families were there, as well as all the names on the scene, including Craig Chaquico, the hot, young guitarist of the Jefferson Starship. So we really had something to prove that night.

Baboo Pierre, the colorful Rastafarian percussionist from the David Lindley Band (El Rayo X) was playing with us. He was a fabulous musician who always referred to himself in the third person. "Baboo hungry," or "Baboo tired."

After the first tune, Ed stepped up to the mike to welcome all the friends, fans, and family. He was talking and suddenly, Baboo grabbed the microphone out of his hands and started repeating over and over again, "People, do you know what I want? People, do you know what I want?" It was an uncomfortable moment, until just as suddenly, Baboo passed out and hit the deck, unconscious. We didn't know what to do, so finally we dragged him to the back of the stage right behind the bandstand and finished the set.

Apparently, Baboo had eaten a few magic mushrooms prior to the gig and "came on" at the exact wrong moment. After the set, all the friends and family came backstage to visit, and Baboo was still rolling around, semi-unconscious and flailing. Everybody had to step over him as we all talked about how good the show was. As if it were normal . . . musicians!

Ah, the seventies . . . Put the natural craziness of musicians together with a whole bunch of drugs, and eventually it's going to hit the rocks. Truly, the music culture back then was far different from today, where most everybody thinks and acts like a professional and is focused on moving up the ladder. We thought it would just fall into place, but mostly it just fell apart.

But even as my musical career was moving in fits and starts, my proximity to all the "hitters" in town started dictating my future. One day I received a phone call from a "Robbie," in response to my ad in the *LA Times*. I gave him my address, and he came over to my apartment and was very impressed with all the instruments I had for sale.

He identified himself as Robbie Robertson from the Band. I was a big fan of the Band and still am. But at the time I didn't know what Robertson looked like, so I had to take his word for it. That day Robbie bought a vintage Martin, as well as a Fender Stratocaster from me. He said he would tell some friends about me, because he had never seen

Norman with Joni Mitchell at Norm's first apartment in Sherman Oaks. (Photo by Marlene Harris)

so many great vintage instruments in one place. At my apartment, you could barely walk through the door. There were guitars, amplifiers, and basses everywhere.

The following week, Robbie called again and asked if he could bring a friend over. I said sure. We made an appointment, and Robbie came over with a friend—Bob Dylan. Bob purchased a beautiful three-point blond Gibson F-4 mandolin from me, as well as a stunning 1953 Fender Blackguard Telecaster.

As a side note, I had purchased the Telecaster from a guitarist who was part of a traveling combo that toured with The Three Stooges. Apparently to go with their live comedy act, they carried this band to add variety to their show.

48

Norman with Bob Dylan in the back of Norm's first store. (Photo by Norman Harris)

So the next week, Robbie called again to ask if he could bring some other friends. Of course I said yes, and this time he showed up with Joni Mitchell, Robben Ford, and Tom Scott. They were recording the album, *Court and Sparks*, and they needed some inspiration. Joni bought a 1944 Herringbone D-28 acoustic. I had several at the time, and she played them and picked out the one she liked best. I think some of my guitars still have those weird tunings that she used. Robben Ford bought a beautiful 1959 Gibson ES-345TD Sunburst with a stop tailpiece. Tom Scott came just to hang out.

I owe a great debt to Robbie Robertson. He basically put me on the map, and by word of mouth, my business began to grow.

The following week Bob Dylan wanted to see another guitar of mine.

I had opened up a storage unit at a place called Beverly Hills Moving and Storage on Haskell Avenue in the San Fernando Valley. Bob came to my place, and we drove over to the storage unit. Bob was driving this older Cadillac with a ripped-up vinyl top. It was anything but classic, and more like a beater.

Bob had brought along his giant bullmastiff named Baby. So, we were in the front seat, and Baby was in the back drooling on both of us. I remember we pulled up to a red light, and a young couple pulled up next to us. They looked at us then their eyes grew wide as they saw it was Bob Dylan driving. Then they gave the raggedy Cadillac and the dog a once-over and shook their heads, deciding "nah, it can't be Dylan."

Meanwhile Ed Robles was also meeting me at my storage unit. We needed to get our Acoustic 360 bass amp out of storage for our next gig. Bob was standing by his Cadillac when Ed pulled up in his old Ford truck, and we needed to load the Acoustic 360 in the back. These were big and heavy amps. Bob was at the bottom of the loading dock, and I was above trying to lower the amp. Bob looked on and I said, half jokingly, "So what are you waiting for?"

Bob helped us load the amp into the truck. I really think he liked the fact that we treated him like a regular guy. So many people are in awe of Bob and don't know how to act around him.

8

EDDIE'S CUSTOM STRAT

N ot all my dealings here in Los Angeles have been with superstars. Some of the rarest and most valuable instruments I've found were owned and used by regular working-type musicians.

Few people know that Southern California was the hub of western swing music in the late forties and fifties. Partly because of the huge migration of southerners here during the Great Depression, but also because it fused dance music with lighthearted, earthy tunes and hot guitar, western swing was extremely popular. Its stars, the notorious Spade Cooley, Jimmy Bryant (the fastest guitarist on the planet, more about him later), and Hank Penny also got a ton of exposure from the new medium of television.

Today it's hard to believe that western swing was once viewed as modern, even space-aged music. But it was, and many musicians and guitar makers were drawn to each other for that reason, each wanting to be a part of the newest trends.

Down in Fullerton, Orange County, a man named Leo Fender was designing and manufacturing the most cutting edge, futuristic assembly-line guitars. They would soon be associated with all types of western music, and beyond.

Eddie O'Clethero was the true definition of a working musician. He had been a New Jersey–born society and pop bandleader during the thirties and forties. But in the late forties, he saw his livelihood slowly drying up. All the gigs were going to cats wearing ten-gallon hats and playing steel guitars and fiddles. Overnight, he transformed himself into western swing bandleader "Eddie Cletro," dumped his clarinets for fiddles, and renamed his band the Roundup Boys. This dual personality led to his being known as the "Sinatra of the Sagebrush." He was very active in the local scene here, opening for Spade Cooley, being the house band on local TV shows, and had a prolific recording career on Columbia, Lariat, Imperial, Decca, Viper, and Sage and Sand labels.

I found Eddie through one of my Musician's Union Local 47 roster cold calls in the early seventies. My line to him was that I was a player/collector who was interested in any older, high-quality Gibson, Fender, and Martin guitars or any other exceptional American-made instruments.

Eddie told me, "I have an older Fender Stratocaster." Immediately, he had my interest. When I asked him to describe it, he said, "It's kind of off-white in color with a dark neck." Not knowing whether the old guy was misremembering stuff, I figured it was an early-1960s Stratocaster with a white finish that was turning yellow in color with age.

I made an appointment with Eddie to see the guitar the next day. He told me he worked at the KTLA television station in Hollywood and would bring the guitar with him to work. To me, this was like prospecting for gold. Who knows what this old "cowboy" might have stashed away?

I drove onto the lot and was escorted upstairs to where Eddie was working. He was a good-looking man, with a quick smile and easy demeanor. I could see how his warm personality had contributed to his success in Hollywood. He told me the guitar was downstairs in the parking lot, in his car's trunk. As we headed down to the car, as usual I was boiling with anticipation.

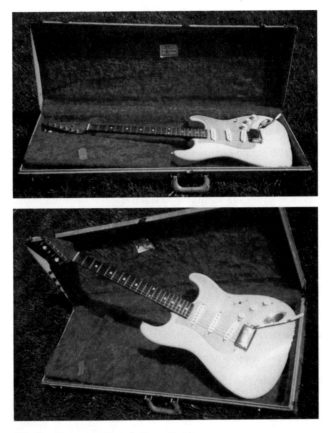

Eddie Cletro Stratocaster. (Photos by Norman Harris)

On the way down, Eddie told me that he had been the bandleader for a western-themed music television show called, *Los Angeles Hayride*, back in the late fifties. He and Leo Fender were old buddies, and Leo gave him the guitar to use on the show.

We arrived at his Cadillac and he popped open the trunk. I was initially puzzled when I saw a clean tweed case there. My first impression was that this could not be the original case or at best, the guitar was a 1959 or 1960 slab board white Stratocaster.

When the case popped open, I almost fell over. I had never seen anything like this Strat. The first thing that stuck out was that it was

53

in desert-sand finish and sported a gold anodized pickguard. That finish was primarily used on 1950s Musicmasters and Duosonics, not Strats. I'd only seen pickguards like that on 1950s Precision Basses, Musicmasters, and Duosonics. But its most unusual feature was an all-rosewood neck! In the late sixties, the all-rosewood Telecaster featured an all-rosewood neck and body, but I'd never seen a full rosewood neck so early. And the serial number plate placed it at the year 1957! I had no reason to doubt that the guitar was totally original.

Was this the first Fender guitar to have an all-rosewood neck? I asked him the story behind the guitar. Eddie told me that he made it clear to Leo that he'd like a Strat, but "Something different. Something that would stand out on TV." Well, this guitar was different, all right. This was a Fender one of a kind.

As a professional musician, Eddie was unsentimental about the guitar. He was more than happy to sell it for cold hard cash—$2,800 worth, and that was a lot of money at the time! And I was more than excited to pay it, though I tried to play it cool.

I immediately ran to my friend Albert Molinaro's Guitar's R Us store in Hollywood. We both gazed at the guitar in amazement. We opened the guitar up to check the pickups and solder joints, and discovered everything was correct and not tampered with.

I kept the guitar for many years and ultimately showed it to my friend John English, the well-known master builder at the Fender custom shop. John urged me to do a small run of reissues of the guitar. John made several, and I believe down the road there were a few others made by other master builders at Fender.

Over the years, people tried to get me to part with the Eddie Cletro Strat, but I was reluctant—it was one of those special guitars that affirmed my passion for collecting.

When my first book, Norman's *Rare Guitars: 30 Years of Guitar*

Collecting, came out, the Strat was, of course, featured. An East Coast collector contacted me, wanting to take it off my hands. Now, there had been two prior guitars that he asked me to hold for him, which, after a period of time, he backed out of. I reminded him that he blew off his last two commitments. I told him the only way that I would know that he was serious would be if he came to me, cash in hand. The guitar was pretty expensive, so I really didn't believe that our conversation was going to go any further.

Three days later, a package arrived at my door. It was the full price for the guitar in cash. Along with the package came a surprise—the FBI, wanting to know why someone transported that much cash to me!

I showed the agents my book, explained what had happened, and told them I hadn't really thought the guy was serious, but apparently he was. They probably investigated and realized I was telling them the truth. It did scare the hell out of me and really caught me by surprise. As you know, I'm not looking for any run-ins with the law!

In the rare guitar business, you always have to take buyers seriously. If he didn't back out of other transactions, I'm sure I wouldn't have made such a strange request, but I guess it all worked out in the end. When I look back at an experience like this, it reminds me of how determined I was to unearth guitar treasures. They were out there, and they are still out there. It must be the same feeling Jacques Cousteau felt when he discovered a shipwrecked treasure. What was merely a tool to Eddie Cletro was treasure to me, and that's not a bad thing.

9

CRASH CORRIGANVILLE

History is a funny thing. Many artists who were obscure during their lifetimes become highly valued decades, if not centuries, later. The painter Vincent van Gogh is the most well known example of this.

You might have your own ideas about how much art was produced through the Los Angeles entertainment industry, but you can't deny its popularity. Even B movie actors, long forgotten by so many people, hold a place in the heart of our culture.

When I was a kid, cowboy movies and TV shows were everywhere. We couldn't get enough of them. And so many of those cowboys had guitars—Gene Autry and Roy Rogers started the whole "singing" cowboy subgenre, and soon every cowboy rode, shot, and plucked their way through the Old West. Even the guys who could barely sing had to have a guitar!

In 1972, I spotted an ad in the *San Fernando Valley Daily News* classified section. It read, "Estate Sale Furniture, Antiques, Guitar, etc., for sale." I called the phone number and spoke with a man who identified himself as Ray.

When I asked about the guitar, he said it was a Gibson Super Jumbo 200. "I am asking $125 for the guitar."

I said, "I'll be right over."

Ray Corrigan Gibson 1937 SJ-100/200.
(Photo courtesy of Hank Risan)

He said, "You better hang on. There's something you should know. You may not want this guitar. It has my name inlaid on the fingerboard."

Now, even back then, I knew that originality was important with these old instruments. Any customization would affect the guitar's value, sometimes in catastrophic ways.

He continued on. "You see, I was a cowboy star for Republic Pictures in the thirties and forties. I made a whole bunch of movies with John Wayne and Smiley Burnett as 'The Three Mesquiteers.' Gibson gave me the guitar."

That definitely perked my interest.

Ray also explained that he had owned a large piece of property called Corriganville and that almost all the Western movies and TV shows in the fifties were filmed there. But now he was moving out of town and wanted to lighten up on his possessions.

Ray then inquired if I had ever heard of him or knew who he was. Being from Florida, I hadn't, but I didn't want to hurt his feelings, so I said I was quite familiar with him and Corriganville, and I would be honored to own his guitar. He was very pleased by this. I didn't realize that any career in Hollywood, no matter how B, would always be a point of pride.Ray gave me his address in the Valley, and I sped over there as fast as possible, wondering about his Gibson. The J-200 has always been the quintessential cowboy guitar, with its super-jumbo body and ornate pickguard and inlays. It seemed the cowboys were always playing that kind of guitar, and it has remained popular throughout the years.

When I arrived, Ray greeted me heartily and pulled out the guitar. A closer look at it revealed that it had mahogany sides and back, instead of rosewood or maple, which meant it was a J-100. The guitar had an ebony fingerboard with his name, "Ray Corrigan," inlaid on it. It had features of both a J-100 and J-200. This instrument was obviously custom-made for him and very special. This had to be a one of a kind.

Ray also pulled out postcards of Corriganville, which he wanted me to have, as well as stationery from Republic Pictures. In a sense, he was entrusting me with his own history, even though he'd never met me before. I later found out that Corriganville was his ranch in Simi Valley that was used as a location for many westerns, including *Fort Apache*, as well as the TV series *The Adventures of Rin Tin Tin*, and *The Lone Ranger*. Ray had the foresight to use the ranch as a western theme park in the late forties, equipped with stuntmen and gunslingers, which was said at its peak to have over 22,000 visitors a day! (This was long before Disneyland.)

But, as with many folks, Ray's career wound down and, after a couple of marriages and a couple of divorces, he sold the ranch to Bob Hope in the late sixties. Hope subdivided and developed the land, and made a killing off it. Thankfully, some of Ray's movie sets are still standing at Corriganville Park in Simi Valley.

———

I met him a few years before he moved to Oregon, where he eventually died in 1976. This was still early on in my career. I knew I had acquired something very special, but I really wasn't aware of how important this guitar really was. I kept the instrument for about twenty years and never had any intention of selling it. It appeared in the book by Tom Wheeler *American Guitars*, which was the bible of vintage guitars for many years. It also appeared in numerous other publications. It became well known that I owned this gorgeous instrument. But I had always assumed Ray Corrigan was just a footnote in Hollywood, an obscure minor player from the forgotten era of B-Westerns.

One day I received a call from someone at the Gene Autry Western Museum. They were aware that I owned this guitar and asked if I would loan it to the museum for an exhibition entitled Western Serenade. The exhibit was to honor all those singing cowboys, and Ray's Gibson would be on display alongside Gene Autry's and Roy Rogers's guitars. Also included in the display were other artifacts that appeared in early Western movies. They asked me if I had any other memorabilia, and I remembered the postcards from Corriganville.

I agreed to loan Ray's stuff to the event. I was invited to the museum and was brought down to the basement where all of the Gene Autry guitars were residing. This was such a great honor, and I was blown away to see and play the greatest Western guitars in the world.

Before me was Gene Autry's J-200. It was gorgeous and in wonderful condition, with fancy rope binding and Gene's name on the fingerboard. I also got to play Gene's Martin 000-45 and several other rare gems that very few people were permitted to hold and strum. They were wonderful time capsules of a more innocent and optimistic era.

The day of the event was fantastic. It seemed like everybody connected with the world of cowboys and guitars was there. Les Paul, who began his career as country picker "Rhubarb Red," was there, as well as numerous luminaries.

I was approached by many people who wanted to know all about my encounters with, and impressions of, Ray. In fact, it seemed like the game of history had dealt him a full house. People were fascinated by him and B-Western history. I found out from a film buff that Ray had ended his career literally in a gorilla suit, playing an ape in another B Hollywood picture. The film buff said that Ray had originally been a physical fitness instructor and trainer to Hollywood actors. That's how he broke in. His nickname, "Crash," was a holdover from his football playing days. The film buff also told me that the Corrigan ranch foreman, who had an affair with Ray's wife, ended up marrying her and killed the actor who portrayed Alfalfa on *Our Gang*, Carl Dean Switzer, in their home when Switzer showed up drunk and asking for money! What price, Hollywood?

Thankfully, my friend Robb Lawrence interrupted us before I heard any more gory details in order to introduce me to Les Paul, which was a thrill. We talked Les Paul guitars, of course, and I got a picture with Les, Marlene, me, and my daughter, Sarah, who was six years old at the time. The photo is on display at my house, and it's something I treasure. Les played beautifully at the event, and it was certainly a night to remember.

At the event, I was approached by a friend from Northern California who was a dealer/collector of fine guitars. He asked me if I would be willing to sell Ray's guitar. I told him it really was not for sale. He said, "I'll give you $50,000 for it." I was sorely tempted, but I didn't want to jump the gun and say yes. I hemmed and hawed. With that he said, "I'll make you one final offer, $75,000."

I said, "You just bought yourself a guitar." I really had no intention of selling it, but this was a lot of money. This was in the early nineties, and $75,000 may have set a record for any Gibson flat-top acoustic at that time.

The bottom line is, we all have our obsessions. The fact that this was Ray's guitar had special significance to my collector/dealer friend. Maybe he loves those old movies, or maybe they just remind him of his cowboy-loving youth. But, in the final analysis, sometimes we all want to get our hands on a little bit of history, even if it's purely "B."

10

NORM'S
IN HOLLYWOOD

I originally came to Los Angeles with my band, because it was the hub of the music industry. I had no idea that the film business would play a large role in putting my vintage guitar business on the map.

I really was at the right place at the right time.

Back in the seventies, the general public was still clueless about the difference between vintage and contemporary guitars. And that went for the film producers, as well. To them, all guitars were interchangeable. It seemed that none of them even considered having period correct guitars in films important. They must have figured that not enough people played guitar or were not aware of how guitar construction and design had changed over the years.

Prop houses didn't consider how inappropriate guitars featured in films might throw an entire scene off-balance, just like seeing an automobile that is not time correct in a period movie. When you see a film like *Field of Dreams*, the old-style baseball uniforms and vintage gloves really give the film credibility.

Unfortunately, that same attention to detail didn't seem to apply to guitars. Having Gary Busey playing a large headstock Fender Stratocaster in 1978's *The Buddy Holly Story* was a glaring mistake. At the time, it probably seemed insignificant, but as time has gone on, it defi-

Bound for Glory movie. (United Artists/Photofest)

nitely detracts from the reality of the movie. That big CBS-era Strat headstock would make any guitar enthusiast uncomfortable!

Among my first customers at my little shop on 6753 Tampa Avenue was David Carradine, as well as his brothers, Keith and Bobby. All three of them had some measure of success in Hollywood. They were LA natives whose father, John Carradine, was a legendary film actor. They were all good musicians—Keith had a Top 40 hit from the film *Nashville*, and David had a special interest in old guitars, which eventually led him to me.

David was an odd guy, but his quirkiness had worked in his favor on the smash TV show *Kung Fu*, which ran from 1972 to 1975. His career was flying high when we met. At a later date, David became well known for the film trilogy, *Kill Bill*, which was produced by Quentin Tarantino.

I remember one time David came into the store carrying a huge, five-gallon water bottle, the kind that would dispense water brands like Arrowhead or Sparkletts. It was totally disgusting looking, filled with mud, tree branches, bugs, and even a dead snake at the bottom. I wasn't sure what he was going to do with this concoction. Possibly use it as a topical ointment? I approached the bottle, and it smelled terrible. I couldn't even get too close. "What the heck's that for?" I inquired. David just smiled, hoisted it up, and took a big swig out of it! Everybody gasped. He assured us this was an ancient Chinese remedy.

In mid-1975, David showed up at the store super-excited. He told me he just got the role of Woody Guthrie in the movie *Bound for Glory*. It was a really prestigious production, to be directed by Hal Ashby, who'd just had a huge hit with *Shampoo*, starring Warren Beatty.

We talked about how the film would take place in the Dust Bowl era. David was determined to make it feel authentic by using time-correct instruments throughout the entire film and wanted me to help. We had several meetings conferring about the instruments that were to be used. We agreed that several wartime-era Banner Gibson acoustics would be used, as well as prewar Martins, upright basses, and vintage drum sets and microphones.

As far as I know, this was the very first film to go out of its way to make instruments period appropriate. Over and over, we went through many choices to make every scene feel authentic. Some instruments had to show lots of wear, while others needed to be clean to be used as Woody's career progressed. Obviously, 1975 was long before all the manufacturers even considered making reissues of vintage instruments that were detail correct, so we had to find time-correct instruments and sprinkle them throughout the movie ourselves. It was a lot of fun. If you've ever seen the film, it really captures the mood of the late thirties to early forties, and feels very authentic.

The movie almost got it all correct.

At the very end of the film, David, as Woody Guthrie, is seen using a Mossman acoustic guitar, which was very noticeable by its pickguard

shape and other details. Mossman was a small guitar maker that produced guitars in the seventies. This was the only instrument used in the
movie that was glaringly time incorrect. To this day, I'm not sure why
David chose to use this guitar (probably some agreement with Mossman). I was very proud of what we did throughout the film, but I was
in shock at seeing Woody playing a Mossman acoustic at the end of the
film! It was very jarring, after all the considerable research we had done.

Over the years, I've dealt with David and his brothers quite a few
times. His son, Max, even took lessons at our store. The Mossman
question was one he never really answered, and he took it to his grave.
Aside from this one mistake, I really believe this film could be in the
Guinness Book of Records as the first film to try to be authentic in its use
of guitars, and I'm proud of my involvement.

<hr>

By 1976, Robbie Robertson had been crucial in building my clientele.
There really was no other place in Los Angeles at the time to find a
large selection of vintage instruments, and he spread the word to his
friends that he had found a good source. So when he came to me with
a proposal, I was all ears.

Last Waltz movie. (United Artists/Photofest)

He explained that the Band had been playing together for sixteen years, touring constantly, and it was time to call it quits. He had spoken with his buddy, film director Martin Scorcese, about doing a final concert with the Band. They had worked with and befriended so many acts that he thought it could be cool to incorporate all of those top acts into a one-night-only concert. Some of the people who would be featured were Bob Dylan, Joni Mitchell, Muddy Waters, Neil Diamond, Neil Young, Eric Clapton, Dr. John, the Staple Singers, Ringo Starr, and many others.

Robbie and Marty were determined—they wanted *The Last Waltz* to be the best documentary ever of their generation. If you ask me, I think it succeeded above and beyond all expectations. It is an incredible document of a specific place and time.

Robbie asked me if I would supply instruments for the film, and because they had such a strong budget, he asked to buy many of the instruments that were in my collection at the time! Because he had been to my warehouse quite a bit, he must've had his eye on my best stuff. He had previously purchased many guitars from me, including a 1954 Fender Stratocaster, a Blackguard Telecaster, some excellent acoustics, and a number of pre-CBS Fender amplifiers, including a couple of four-by-ten Bassman amps. I knew he coveted my 1919 Martin Koa Wood 00-45K (I believe the only one ever made), as well as my mint 1969 Gibson Citation number one. This guitar was unusual because it was shown at the NAMM Show (National Association of Musical Merchants) and was extremely rare in natural blond finish. Another instrument Robbie had his eye on was a 1958 Gibson Double-Neck electric six string, and an eight-string mandolin, a one-of-a-kind special order in cherry finish with an unusual soft, round cutaway.

Because I was such a fan of so many of the acts, including the Band, I agreed. Robbie and I settled on a price and we proceeded to my ware-

Fender Stratocaster. (Photo by Jen Angkahan)

house to get the instruments. We had to restring and set them up so they were ready for play. Robbie had very good taste and cherry-picked some of my finest guitars and amps, which meant I needed to find more, immediately. However, I felt very privileged to attend a number of the rehearsals for the film at the Band's compound in Malibu, during which time various substances flowed freely.

They were some of the finest musicians ever, and I was knocked out by all, especially Garth Hudson and Richard Manuel (both unbelievable keyboard players). I'd always loved Levon's drumming and vocals. Actually all the vocals in the band were very stylized and very authentic. Their songwriting was so strong and real, it felt as though you were listening to music from a previous century. I used to call it "civil war funk."

In the movie, Levon played the double neck guitar/mandolin. Robbie played the citation, the Martin, and the Stratocaster that I had previously sold him, with a back line of some of the coolest tweed amps around. Over the years, many people have asked me particulars about the Stratocaster Robbie played in the film, because it doesn't sound like your normal Strat. Robbie was fond of putting Gibson Melody Maker pickups in his Stratocasters and wiring them together to act like humbuckers. It's cool because his tone was much beefier than your standard single-coil Strat.

It was a magical event. Dr. John killed it doing "Such a Night." Joni was mesmerizing on her legendary tune "Coyote," from her *Court and Sparks* album. The Staple Singers were also a personal favorite, with Pop Staples playing some very hip and understated guitar. Bob Dylan was great as usual, and was particularly outstanding in the finale with "I Shall Be Released." Muddy Waters was in top form. Eric Clapton did some serious gunslinging with Robbie on "Further on Up the Road." Neil Young and all the rest of the performers truly stepped it up, because no one wanted to be outdone by all the talent waiting in the wings.

The Band showed everyone that they were a magnificent back-up band to all the other stars. They delved deep into their history while

Back to the Future movie. (Universal/Photofest)

many folks were still vibrant and alive. Sadly, so many of them—Muddy Waters, Pops Staples, Paul Butterfield, Richard Manuel, Garth Hudson, Rick Danko, and Levon Helm are gone now.

I attended the film's premiere at the Cinerama Dome in Hollywood, and many of the film stars were also in attendance. It was a bittersweet but fitting farewell to a wonderful time and a brilliant band. It was intended to be a masterpiece, and it delivered on all fronts. As the years go on, *The Last Waltz* still looms large.

Robbie ended up keeping a number of instruments and still owns them to this day. Recently C. F. Martin & Company reissued a replica of the Koa Wood Martin acoustic flat-top that Robbie owns and used in the movie. After the film, Robbie starred in and produced a picture called *Carny*. It was an authentic look at the lives of carnival performers. I also recommend checking this one out. Some of the musical performances in the film are terrific.

———

Over the years, movie producers and directors began to realize it made sense to make guitars time correct in film. Luckily, I was thought to be one of the experts in the field. Sometimes even the best of intentions get ignored by the film's art director.

In 1984, members of the Warner Brothers' prop department contacted me and told me they were working on a film that would take place in 1955. They wanted something that looked slightly futuristic, and I thought that possibly a Gibson ES-5 Switchmaster with all its knobs and P-90 pickups might be just the thing.

I showed the prop master the guitar. He agreed that it looked cool and different, and thought it would work perfectly. The guitar was in excellent condition and at the time had a price tag of $2,100. I suggested that the film buy the guitar, but the prop master said they would be happy to rent it for the sum of $300 per week. I agreed, and the guitar went off to the *Back to the Future* movie set.

They originally planned on renting the guitar for one or two weeks. After nine weeks, I told them they'd be better off just buying the guitar, but the prop master said not to worry, the film had a large budget and it didn't really matter. After the tenth week, I received a call from the prop department telling me they hadn't even opened the case yet. He said not to worry, they would pay me for the ten-week rental, but the art director had changed his mind and wanted something different. He was now thinking they wanted a red guitar with a whammy or tremolo bar.

I informed him that nothing fit the bill that would be time correct for 1955. He said the art director didn't mind taking artistic license and wanted to know what red guitars with a whammy bar I had in stock. I showed him several guitars. One was a Gretsch 6120, another a Gretsch red jet series guitar, and the last was an early 1960s Gibson ES-345TDC with a Bigsby tremolo. After showing the pictures to the art director, they decided on the Gibson ES-345TDC.

I reminded him that this guitar did not exist in 1955, but they insisted on using the Gibson. It sat in the prop truck for four weeks before finally being used. They could have purchased the guitar several times over for the amount of the rental, but this never seemed to bother them, which is one of the many positives when you rent stuff to Hollywood—money is no object!

After the filming concluded, I was paid for the rental, which to me seemed insane, but everybody was happy.

Three weeks later, they contacted me again saying they needed to rent the guitar for inserts and closeup shots. This time they kept the guitar for an additional three weeks. This seemed so crazy to me because it was a complete disregard for money, but everybody was happy in the end. I kept the guitar for quite a while and was happy to see it featured in the movie.

In terms of artistic liberty, the glaring violation of period realism in that movie never really commanded any negative attention. Maybe because it was a time travel, sci-fi movie, they could get away with that kind of stuff. In a movie like *Bound for Glory*, it would be more noticeable. Maybe it's just for the "guitar geeks" to know and point out. Like they say in Hollywood, "The truth is no excuse . . . " (for a bad story).

A few years later, they contacted me again saying they were going to do *Back to the Future Part II*, and would need the guitar once again. My answer was a resounding, "*Yes.*" By then, they were married to this guitar, and it made an extremely profitable deal for me. This time, because the movie was such a sensation, they didn't want to mess around by using anything but the original guitar. And because it was a sequel, money truly was no object. I realized just how lucrative renting to the movies could be. When in Rome . . .

A year or two later, I ended up selling the guitar to an old childhood friend, Richard Glick. I made a tidy profit, because it was a well-known movie guitar. I know that Richard later resold the guitar for quite a bit more. I should've held onto it longer. Well, sometimes you hit homers, and sometimes you hit singles.

The guitar is an important piece of movie memorabilia because the film was such a blockbuster and is rightly viewed as a modern classic— even with the period-incorrect ES-345!

The film business is, at its essence, a crapshoot. Nobody knows what will be successful, or what films, at the end of the day, will become classics. If you ask me, I'll tell you which ones I like, but I can't tell you if they'll ever become a part of the everyday language of our culture.

Chris Guest was one of my original customers at the old store. He was a folkie who had bought a number of acoustic instruments from

This Is Spinal Tap movie. (Embassy Pictures/Photofest)

me. One was a prewar Martin D-28, and another was a 1920s Gibson F-4 mandolin.

One day he told me about a movie he was going to star in and co-produce, called *This Is Spinal Tap*. His term for the movie was a "mockumentary," and it was to be loosely based on the rise and fall of an early heavy metal band. The story had all the usual conflicts rock bands have, including the women and managers pulling the band members apart. The members of the band are clueless; they can play their own music but are oblivious to other commonplace, day-to-day things that the rest of the population has to deal with. The trajectory of the group is from playing huge concert venues to being co-billed with a puppet show at the Holiday Inn.

Chris told me, "There is no real script," meaning that each scene has a context but would be ad-libbed by all the actors. The premise was about "producer" Rob Reiner directing a documentary on the rise and fall of the group. Michael McKeon and Harry Shearer of *Saturday Night Live* would be in the group playing second guitar and bass. Others ap-

73

pearing in the film would be Fran Drescher (this was one of her very first roles) and Paul Shaffer from the *Late Show with David Letterman* fame. The premise sounded very funny. It was 1981. MTV was a mere blip. Reality television didn't exist. I don't recall any other "mockumentary" ever being done.

Chris asked me if I would be interested in supplying all the instruments to the film. I agreed, and we had several meetings discussing what instruments were to be used. There would be instruments that the band would be playing, as well as a scene where Chris (as character Nigel Tufnel) showed off his massive guitar collection. Chris was very knowledgeable, and he helped me hand select instruments that were to be used in this scene. What I find interesting is that I never knew Chris to be an electric player, but he had a very good grasp of what was really cool in the electric world.

For the film, Chris purchased a 1954 Gibson Les Paul Goldtop in excellent condition with a stop tailpiece. Michael purchased an early Gibson SG Les Paul Special. This guitar had an original white finish, two Gibson P-90 pickups, and was also in excellent condition. During the film, these two guitars were of primary use. Other guitars were sporadically used in various scenes, but the two guitars that Chris and Michael purchased were in the major parts of the film. A Marshall amplifier head was used, and they reprinted the numbers to go up to eleven instead of ten. This was a featured gag in the film and, of course, "goes to eleven" has become part of the lexicon of our culture. They figured if ten was good, eleven was even better. In the famed Stonehenge scene, Chris Guest even wore a Norman's Rare Guitars T-shirt. Thank you, Chris!

When it came to the guitar collection scene, we meticulously went through some of my finest guitars. There was a 1959 Gibson Sunburst Les Paul Standard with an absolutely killer top. When referring to this

74

guitar in the film, Chris said, "It has so much sustain that you could go out and have a bite to eat and the guitar would still be sustaining." Some others used in the guitar collection scene were a 1950 Fender Broadcaster serial number 0022, which I still own; a late-1950s Gibson double neck 6-12; a beautiful blond Super 400 CES; and my Fender Electric Bass VI in seafoam green. This instrument was dead mint with the original hangtags. In one scene, Chris said to Rob Reiner that this guitar was so mint it was not to be played. When Rob pointed at the guitar, Chris said, "Don't even point at it, don't even look at it!" I later sold this Bass VI and had severe seller's remorse over letting it go.

Chris invited me to a screening of the film, which I thoroughly enjoyed. Watching the actors ad-lib their lines was extremely interesting. They were so creative, tossing out different ideas each time. Some of the things I saw that did not make the film were hilarious. Everyone

Fender 1950 Broadcaster.
(Photos by Jen Angkahan)

seemed to have a great time on the set. I attended several different screenings of the film. Each one was different, with scenes being added or deleted until the final cut was made. I felt the screening I attended just prior to the film's release was the best. This was not the final cut. The film has proved to be a comedy classic. Everybody loves *Spinal Tap*, and it was a gas being a part of it.

I invited a friend of mine from England named Chris Trigg to one of the screenings. I think he took a little offense at the film and said, "This will not go over well in England." I believe he was proven wrong. The film is appreciated the world over and was even re-released years later. The film is regularly seen on cable and almost every rock and roll fan worth his salt has seen the film many times over.

Throughout the years, Chris Guest has done several other films with a musical element. The film *A Mighty Wind* was actually more true to Chris's first love, folk music, and I'm proud to say that we supplied instruments to that film as well. The film featured acoustic instruments, and once again Chris was very specific as to what instruments were to be used. A variety of Martin and Gibson acoustics, as well as banjos, mandolins, and upright basses were used in the film.

Another film Chris did at a later time called *For Your Consideration* did not have a musical theme except for one part of the film, and I was once again honored to supply a wonderful Gibson Banner flat-top acoustic to the film. I will always appreciate Chris's loyalty to me and will always be there if he needs me again.

One line that appeared in a rare *Spinal Tap* magazine that I felt was one of Chris's most brilliant quotes was, "You know that Spinal Tap is great because we play really loud. All those jazz musicians play so low that you just have to take their word for it that they are good."

As usual, you never really know which are the films that will take hold and last throughout time. That's what makes it fun.

11

PLAN
B

E ven with all the action I had selling instruments and my head-
spinning proximity to world-class artists, I was still pursuing my
own music. LA in the seventies was still a place where you could gig
steadily, if you had a solid band.

Ed Robles (AKA Gabriel Black) and I joined forces with the Juke
Rhythm Band, which included the late great John "Juke" Logan on blues
harp and piano, my buddy Dan Duehren on bass, Joe Yuele on drums,
and the phenomenal Rick Vito on lead guitar. Thus, we became the Angel
City Rhythm Band.

Angel City Rhythm Band. (Photo by Norman Harris)

Everyone in the group was musically very strong. Our sound was a mix of James Brown–style funk grooves with an overlay of blues harp. Juke Logan was an excellent writer, and we all took turns singing lead. In retrospect, though, not having one lead singer probably made it hard for record companies to know exactly how to sell us. Our vocals would go in different directions almost song by song depending on who was singing.

Our versatility didn't affect our popularity in the clubs. We were busy. We were the house band at a club on Van Nuys Boulevard called The Rock Corporation. When Tom Petty and the Heartbreakers first formed, they didn't have any gigs, and we were able to secure them a gig there before they began to play a lot of original tunes. They mainly played Rolling Stones cover tunes and other rock hits.

———

I'll never forget one particular night at the club. We were in the middle of a tune and one of my friends came running in, yelling, "Marlene's water just broke!" I jumped off the bandstand, tore home in my car, picked her up, and rushed to Cedars. It turned out we jumped the gun by a day. My son, Jordan, was born twenty-four hours later.

Though I was thrilled to become a dad, I was wholly unprepared for the responsibility that goes along with it. Because we were still pretty young, Marlene and I foolishly thought we could still continue living life as we knew it and just bring the baby along with us.

Jordan must've been a few months old when the band got a gig backing up Dobie Gray, a crossover pop soul singer of the seventies. (Any of you remember the number-one hit "Drift Away" or "The in Crowd"?) We played in Vegas and Salt Lake City, and after a gig in Reno, Marlene and I figured we'd drive home with Jordan. Wearing only the clothes we had on our backs, we saddled up my beat-up old

Mercedes at around 2:00 a.m. and hit the road. In a godforsaken place called Miracle City, one of the car's hoses blew, and we came to a halt in the middle of nowhere. It was freezing! We finally made it to a motel, chilled to the bone, but by then Marlene had decided that it was easier to take care of the kid at home. She decided not to travel with the band to our out-of-state gigs.

Another night, Dan Duehren and I were driving the truck back from a gig at a club in Santa Barbara called the Feed Store, when it suddenly ground to a halt. We'd run out of gas. Luckily, Juke Logan had left after us, and he gave us a ride, along with a gas can, to the nearest gas station. It was pretty desolate out there. When we started pumping gas, some freak in a camouflage outfit emerged from the darkness and started giving us "hippies" a bunch of shit. Danny, no stranger to dishing it out, gave the nutjob some lip back. Next thing I knew, the crazy fucker pulled out a rifle, cocked it, and aimed it right at my head. I was high as a kite, and my life flashed before my eyes. I had two kids, (my daughter, Sarah, had just been born) a loving wife, a house, a small business, and here I was—about to die in the middle of nowhere, at the hands of some maniac, for reasons unknown! I loved my art, but I didn't love it enough to die for it. Somehow we talked our way out of it, and even Danny was quiet for the rest of the ride to LA.

Yes, the life of a working musician! Paying for diapers, formula, and baby clothes also reminded me that, popular as we were, the band wasn't really bringing home the bacon. Yet. I had hope though. People really dug us. Quite often, respected musicians around town would show up to where we were playing to check us out. Bonnie Raitt was a regular at the Topanga Corral. All good, until . . . she poached Rick Vito from the band! It was a huge loss and it kind of pulled out the rug from underneath us. Rick was such a charismatic player, singer, and integral writer and instrumentalist for the band, things were never quite the

Norman playing bass with King Cotton at the Santa Barbara Zoo opening event. (Photo by Marlene Harris)

same. After Rick left, my buddy John Paulus came out from Florida to play with us, but Rick's absence was a pretty big hole to fill. We lost momentum.

The Angel City Rhythm Band still played together and occasionally Rick Vito would sit in with us. We were the band of choice for many big name blues artists, but this was considerably after the prime of their careers. We probably backed up Albert Collins about fifty times. He played a 1965 Telecaster Custom with a stripped down finish and always had some kind of sparkly contact paper over the bridge cover. He would turn up his Fender Quad Reverb amp to ten and had a searing, funky tone. He would play everything with a capo in open position, bending and popping those notes with his fingers. His guitar strap was always slung over one shoulder. His expressions during tunes were priceless. He always had a two-hundred-foot guitar cord and would go outside the club onto the street during his solos, and everybody would follow him in. What an original!

We also backed Big Joe Turner and Lowell Folsom on many occa-sions. Other artists we backed up were Eddie "Cleanhead" Vinson, Roy Milton, Margie Evans (from the Johnny Otis Show), Big Mama Thorn-ton, and many others.

For my fortieth birthday, Rick got Marlene to hire these wonderful a capella singers for my birthday party. Rick knew I loved doo-wop, and I was knocked out by these guys. We put them together with R&B singer King Cotton and, lo and behold, we soon had a very tight musical blues and soul band, with some fantastic vocal harmonizing.

The Texas-born King Cotton is not only a dynamite performer but a serious roots and blues archeologist and "true believer." Once he and I got together, it was a true meeting of the minds concerning deep blues, rock and roll, and R&B cuts. We even created a radio show called *King Cotton's (White Blur) Show*. We decided we would only play the best and most obscure songs. Tunes like "That's What Love Will Do for You" by Little Milton, "Thread the Needle" by Clarence Carter, and "That's How Heartaches Are Made" by Baby Washington. I also co-produced a vintage rhythm and blues radio show with the great Billy Vera. Billy is also an amazing singer, guitarist, and showman, and is a vintage rhythm and blues authority. Billy had several hits in the sixties ("With Pen in Hand" and "Country Girl, City Man" with the great Judy Clay). Many years later, he had a monster hit with the tune, "At This Moment." Many album reissues that have been released over the years have had liner notes done by Billy Vera.

When we lost our bass player last minute to a better paying gig, I stood in on bass. We didn't have time to bring someone else in, and I knew the chord changes, the arrangements and, more importantly, how to stay out of the way. Lord knows I had access to fine instruments, so I ended up playing bass in the band for two years. It was some of the most fun I've ever had, musically.

We were the house band at St. Mark's Place in Venice, and many people used to sit in with us—guys like Joe Walsh, Lee Michaels, and my good buddy Frank Stallone.

What happened was our labor of love turned out to be more of a regular gig, as we got booked more and more nights during the week. Now I was in my forties, getting up early to get the newspapers, opening the store, and I could not burn both ends of the candle like when I was young. Because the other musicians in the band needed a steady income, I didn't want to take food out of their mouths, so I stepped aside.

———

I got into the guitar business because I loved music and I dug hanging out with musicians. And luckily, through my last two bands, I got to back up some of the greatest blues players toward the end of their careers when most of them were working as singles and often requested us to back them up.

It was very cool playing with cats like King Cotton because we were students of the classic era. We backed up Bo Didley a number of times toward the end of his career, on the Santa Monica pier and in clubs downtown. We knew that Bo had recorded an album on Chess with the Moonglows (probably the greatest doo-wop group ever), and we had all the arrangements down, including three- and four-part harmonies, which really blew Bo's mind. Bo was used to having pickup bands not knowing his tunes, and once we kicked out "I'm Sorry" and "Didley Daddy," Bo was very impressed with how organized we actually were. He couldn't believe we'd dug out those deep cuts from his past, and he loved it. Bo's daughter was also a super-funky drummer, and she often sat in with us.

Once we did a gig with Bo and the crazed comedian Rudy Ray

Moore, known as the "Dolomite," after a pimp he played in some of those black exploitation pictures from the seventies. Rudy also was a reappearing character on the *White Blur Show*. Rudy was always hysterical! I'll never forget sitting backstage while Rudy and Bo exchanged "dirty dozens," each one upping the other with the insults, like "your mother's so ugly she has to sneak up on a glass of water," stuff like that. All remnants from the Chitlin' Circuit era. Those two had us on the floor they were so damn funny.

One exceptional musician who reinvented himself was the great Johnny "Guitar" Watson. He transformed from jump bluesman to funk pimp in the seventies, turning out catchy hits like "Ain't That a Bitch," and "It's a Real Mother for Ya." Though we never backed him, I used to see him around town at the car wash, driving his customized Stutz Bearcat, dressed in full-on pimp regalia. After he died in 1996, his wife sold me one of his ES-335s and a Strat. I was really excited when she let me have one of Johnny's full-length fur coats! Inside the coat, sewn into the pocket, were the words *Johnny Guitar*. I sold the coat to the incredible New Orleans piano player John Cleary (from Bonnie Raitt's band), and he's been known to wear that coat in one-hundred-degree weather down in N'awlins.

Johnny Guitar Watson was the exception. A lot of these folks were alcoholics, living pretty much hand to mouth. I'll never forget backing up Big Mama Thornton at the Starwood toward the end of her career. She had lost a lot of weight and wore these madras shorts and shirt, and had on a fishing cap. Toward the end of the set, she told the audience, "Big Mama's been real sick lately," and then she passed her fishing cap around, while we played a slow blues. When she put the hat back on her head, all the change and bills fell out all over the floor. She got down on her hands and knees to pick up those dollars and coins. It was heartbreaking.

Like Levon Helm said, "We're not in it for our health. The truth was, the music business had changed radically by the eighties. As those great blues artists passed away, disco and programmed beats and samples took over. With hindsight, I realized that *The Last Waltz* truly was the end of an era. Luckily for me, people still wanted to write songs and perform on guitar!

Gibson 1969 ES-335. (Photo by Jen Angkahan)

12

FOUNDING FATHERS OF FENDER

One of my reasons for laying down stakes here in Los Angeles was its proximity to West Coast guitar manufacturers—mainly Fender Musical Instruments. As the years went on, I picked up many outstanding and unique instruments but was disappointed that I had never gotten anything directly from the "source in the day."

All that changed one day in 1988, when I received a call from a gentleman who was looking to sell some old Fender amps for a fair price. I told him I certainly was very interested. He said his name was Ernest Tavares. Immediately, I felt my pulse quicken!

Any student of Fender knows that brothers Freddie and Ernest Tavares, along with Doc Kauffman, Leo Fender, and a few others, were the original founders of the Fender Electric Musical Instrument Manufacturing Company, back in 1946. It was believed that the brothers were instrumental in the development and design of many of Fender's most iconic models, including the Stratocaster. They were long-time employees and valuable associates of Leo Fender. As musicians themselves, they used to frequent nightclubs and concerts to gather input from local musicians on Fender's innovative designs, and I believe that is part of the reason why those early designs are so enduring—because they're practical as well as beautiful.

What Ernest was selling was a pre-CBS Fender Super Reverb amp and an early Tweed Princeton amp. I assured him that I was aware of who he was, and I would be happy to buy his amps and, as a matter of fact, I'd pay decent money for whatever equipment he wanted to sell. Still sporting his native Hawaiian tan and irrepressible manner, Ernest came by and we closed the deal, all the while talking about the early days of Fender. You have to remember that the late eighties was the era of "hair bands" and Marshall-oriented high-gain EL-84 amps. Ernest's modest 6V6 tweeds were out of style. I think he found it satisfying that I was aware of who he was and was so intrigued by his contribution to the Fender company.

I must have made an impression because a few weeks later, I got a call from Ernest's younger brother, Freddie. Freddie had been an accomplished guitar player, as well as a very successful steel guitar player. As a matter of fact, it became known years later that he had played the steel heard at the beginning of all the Warner Brothers' Looney Tunes *The Bugs Bunny Show* cartoons! That means we all grew up listening to Freddie Tavares. After a pleasant phone call, Freddie invited me to his house, down in the Long Beach area.

When I arrived at his modest home, I casually looked around to see if any of his collection was lying around. Like most musicians, he had a bunch of equipment he'd gathered over the years, but it wasn't immediately noticeable. The first thing he pulled out was an early Rickenbacker frying pan steel guitar. These were some of the first electric guitars ever made and supposedly an influence on Leo Fender, as well as solidbody pioneer Paul Bigsby. As I examined the Rick, I caught a glimpse of a Fender Jazzmaster guitar sitting out of its case behind Freddy's tattered couch. I could only see the top of the guitar's headstock from where I was standing, but I could feel something was different. When he dug the guitar out from behind the couch, I saw it had several unique features. Most unusual was the guitar's maple neck.

Fender 1958 Jazzmaster. (Photos by Jen Angkahan)

I had only seen them with rosewood fingerboards. Two other details were the black anodized pickguard and the desert-sand finish most commonly used on early Musicmasters and Duosonics.

When I asked Freddie about these unusual features, he said, "This was one of the very first Jazzmasters. It's either the first or second ever made." He said they were still trying to decide on what features would be made as standard design. He liked the desert-sand finish and he thought the black anodized guard would be a good contrast to the body finish. He said he preferred the maple neck, but at the time of the guitar's build, they were just introducing necks with a rosewood fingerboard. This guitar had a one-piece all-maple neck like the original Telecaster-style guitars, as well as the early Stratocasters, Musicmasters, and Duosonics.

Because the company was very high on the new rosewood fingerboards that were applied on top of the maple necks, it was decided that all production guitars would have these rosewood fingerboards. Freddie loved my enthusiasm and told me he wanted me to own the guitar—for a price of $2,500. I told him that I would be happy to pay that, which was higher than any Jazzmaster had ever gone for at that time. Today this seems to be an insignificant amount, but at the time it seemed to be hugely overpriced. Believe it or not, back then, Sunburst Les Pauls from the late fifties were going for $10,000 to $12,000, so $2,500 was a lot for a Jazzmaster.

Freddie also pulled out a prototype guitar that he had, a Fender Swinger body with Marauder appointments and a maple neck with a pointed headstock. What made the Marauder design unusual was that the pickups were hidden underneath the pickguard (no pickups visible). The Marauder never really went into production, and there were a few variants on the design. I did see one once with pickups that were exposed. The guitar has a black anodized pickguard with numerous switches on top. Freddie told me that he personally finished the body in black. This again was a guitar that did not exist and never went into production. Of course I purchased the Swinger/Marauder from Freddie as well.

We spoke for a couple hours and, because I was such a fan of the company, he informed me that he also had numerous letters written from him to Leo regarding guitar design, as well as some sample decals from later guitars such as Broncos, Lead I and II, and a few others. He said he was contemplating throwing these out, but if I was interested he would give them to me. Needless to say, I said yes, and still have these letters and decals, as well as the Jazzmaster and the Swinger/Marauder guitar, to this day.

These priceless artifacts are important parts of my personal collection. When I first acquired the Rickenbacker steel guitar, I didn't have much love for any steel guitar, and I sold it shortly afterward. Back then, I didn't even know too much about Freddie's history as a renowned steel guitar player. I'm not even sure if I let the buyer know that it once belonged to Freddie Tavares. Sadly, some time later, after Freddie had passed away, I was contacted by someone from his family asking if they could buy back the Rickenbacker frying pan because that was the instrument he mostly used, and it meant a lot to them. Unfortunately I had to let them know that it was long gone and that I was very sorry about that.

The history of music often goes in trends. The lap steel guitar might as well have been an accordion in the eighties metal years. Only lately has the interest in the history of roots music picked up, and people have researched many important players in the genre. Freddie was that and much more. I knew he was a key figure, but it didn't remove my blinders in preferring the Fender solidbody electrics to his early Rickenbacker steel guitar.

In my history as a guitar dealer, sometimes I have sold things a little too quickly, which I later regretted. I didn't realize what an important piece of music memorabilia I had in my possession—perhaps a missing link in the chain of early lap steel solidbodies that led to the Stratocaster and beyond.

13

THE RIGHT TIME TO SELL

W hen dealing with collectibles, the ultimate question is: When is the right time to sell? Has the market peaked?

Nobody wants to cash out, only to find out later if they'd only held on, they'd be rolling in the clover.

If I only knew!

The laws of economics say that all markets and values are based on supply and demand. Simple, right? When the demand exceeds the supply, the value goes up. If there are ten thousand of something and a million people want one, the price goes up. If there is only one of something and nobody cares, there is little value. This applies to guitars even more so.

Over the years, I have sold so many guitars thinking that I did really well at that time, and for *that time* I did do well. But relative to the price of those exact guitars today, I blew it.

I have a split personality. The businessman in me says, "Don't be the last person holding the bag." The collector in me says, "I love this object and will never let it go!"

In almost every instance that I sold before a peak, I had good reason. Maybe I had to remodel a house, buy a car, diversify some investments. Everything seemed to make sense at the time. Still, I could write an encyclopedia of the guitars I sold that have gone up fiftyfold in value.

Growing up listening to the Beatles, Bob Dylan, James Brown, great jazz artists like Wes Montgomery, George Benson, Django Reinhardt, and great blues artists like Albert King, B.B. King, Little Milton, and Little Beaver (in Miami) has been a crucial part of my life experience. The models that these artists played have meaning to me and all guitar players around the world. In the back of our minds is the thought, "If I only had that specific guitar, maybe I could sound like that!" And then we pursue our version of that sound. That's what it's all about.

Guitars are emotional things for me. They're one of the things America did right. I'm in love with their playability, feel, mojo, whatever you might want to call it. These instruments make music, and music has been a continuous source of inspiration to me.

My old friend Jim Weider loves to check in with me by phone a couple times a year. As time goes on, we talk about our kids and our various age-related ailments, just feeling good to be connected. He always ends the conversation with, "I'm lovin' that 1953, Norm. Thanks mucho."

Ugh. He's referring to the 1953 Blackguard Tele I sold to him for $350. Granted it was the early seventies, and at the time I thought I did very well. Three hundred and fifty dollars was a lot of dough back then!

Like I mentioned in a previous chapter, I sold late-1950s Sunburst Les Pauls for $1,500 to $5,000 a piece. Each time I thought I did great, only to later find out that I jumped the gun in the worst possible way.

You can't live with regrets, but when I think about those fourteen Sunburst Les Pauls I sold, because I got "cold feet." At the least I have provided wonderful investments to a lot of people. Many of my customers have made a lot of money by holding on to their guitars, and one day they may thank me, LOL.

The greatest story about selling at the peak of the market involves my friend Bob Turner in Phoenix, Arizona. Bob started dealing vintage guitars at a very young age, as a teenager. He was a visionary. One day, Bob was trolling the ads in the newspaper in Phoenix, Arizona, and he spotted a Gibson SG Special. He tracked down the guitar, saw it was very clean, and made the deal, happy with his purchase.

While driving home with the SG, Bob passed through an area of town that would later get developed. There were a few run-down older houses there, and as Bob drove by this one house, he saw a young man standing in front of a house playing a guitar. He was driving by quite fast but made a quick about-face, turning around to see what this kid was playing.

It was an odd-looking instrument, very angular. Kind of like those crazy heavy metal guitars the Japanese would later develop.

The year was 1971. The Ibanez guitar company didn't even exist. Bob stopped at the house and saw the kid was playing a guitar that looked pretty interesting—as in Gibson Explorer *interesting*. Hardly anybody knew about the legendary, ultra rare Explorer, but Bob had incredible instincts, and he knew that this could be one of them.

Bob started a conversation with this kid about guitars in general. After taking a closer look, Bob quickly realized this was indeed an original 1958 Explorer. This must have been one of the ones that were shipped in 1963. This one had unusual features; it had a black pickguard and a short maestro vibrato unit. Bob wanted to buy the guitar from this young man, but he had spent all his cash on the SG.

So, Bob figured he'd use whatever bait he had on him. He pulled out the SG and flashed it at the young man. The kid's eyes lit up, and he asked if he could try it.

"Sure," Bob said. The kid took it and started noodling some Clapton licks.

The kid said, "This guitar plays great! Would you consider trading me for my guitar?"

Gibson 1958 Explorer. (Photo by Bob Turner)

Bob tried to control his enthusiasm and said, "Well, I guess so." They made the trade, and I've included the photo of Bob with the guitar in front of that house, all those years ago.

Bob is sixty-three now and is hardly recognizable as the teenager in the photo. (As am I, as you can see in the other photos in the book.) The more I think about it, it just seems damn impossible to imagine. There was actually a time when you could stumble across someone playing an original Explorer in his front yard and trade a P-90-equipped SG for it!

The story isn't over. You know what's coming next. After a few years, Bob sold the guitar for a few thousand dollars. This seemed like a killing at the time.

Except for the fact that these guitars now go for up to a half-million dollars or more!

We now come back to the original question. What was more stupid, the kid's trading the guitar for the SG, or Bob's selling it for only a few thousand dollars? This is the dilemma faced by all guitar dealers and collectors. When is the right time to sell?

After talking with Bob, we both agreed on the answer. We have no regrets. We have led wonderful lives and have had a lot of fun doing this. It has been an honor to have owned these great instruments, even temporarily. We sold them at a time that we felt was right, and now someone else can carry the burden of trying to guess when the guitar market will peak.

Bob is one of the early pioneers of the vintage guitar business. Like myself, Bob has been buying and selling vintage guitars since the late sixties. There are many Bob Turner stories. Many of the stories are legendary. Bob has always been quite a character, and this is one of my favorite remembrances.

One day, a young man came into Bob's store and sold him an inexpensive Rickenbacker solidbody guitar. I believe it was either a Ryder or an Electro. These were subsidiaries of Rickenbackers, their lower-end models.

Bob at the time paid the young man $400 for the guitar. A few weeks later the young man arrived back at Bob's store asking if he could buy back his guitar. Bob said, "Sure, I'll sell it back to you for $500." This was a small and very reasonable profit for Bob's $400 investment.

The young man replied, "I would like to buy the guitar back for $400."

Bob said, "Look, I'm willing to sell it back to you for a minimal profit, but I feel I'm entitled to make something on the guitar."

The young man once again replied, "I would like to buy it back for $400."

Bob said, "Well, then what's in it for me? You're not being reasonable!"

The young man, getting a little angry, said, "No, I want it back for what I sold it for!"

Bob said, "All right, I'll sell it back to you for $450."

The young man once again insisted, "I want it back for the amount I sold it for."

This conversation kept going on, and Bob said, "Okay, come with me behind the store." Bob put the guitar on the step behind the store, pulled out his .45, and blew the guitar to bits. He said, "Now you can have it for nothing." I guess that's one way to end a conversation!

Everybody that knows Bob has stories about him. He's definitely an unusual character, but he is one of my oldest guitar buddies. He can be an acquired taste, but you can't help but love the guy.

———

The businessman in me often buys back guitars I once sold, for much higher prices, because it's a new business opportunity. I have had many customers turn tremendous profits selling me back guitars that I once sold to them.

I have sold Sunburst 1950s Les Paul Standards for $2,500, buying them back ten years later for $25,000, then reselling and re-brokering them for six-figure sums. The same has been true for high-end flat-top acoustics. I once brokered one of the finest Martin prewar D-45s for $7,500. At the time the $7,500 seemed like huge money. The buyer later resold the guitar for over twenty times his investment. I have to look at each deal as a new opportunity.

The market is influenced by many factors. Because the vintage guitar market is an international phenomenon, exchange rates greatly influence prices and demand. When the dollar is weak against foreign currency, it becomes a terrific bargain to buy American goods. At times, instruments were purchased for sixty or seventy cents on the dollar.

The Japanese market is a good case in point. The Japanese have been greatly influenced by American music and musicians. They quickly realized American-made guitars were extremely well made. As prices escalated, they wanted to get in on the action. Japan was the first country outside the United States to recognize the investment opportunity in vintage guitars. When the exchange rates were favorable, these instruments were a great bargain.

Because my father brought the Brother Sewing Machine Corporation to the United States, we always had many Japanese friends, and I have always had a great affinity and respect for the Japanese people.

My store eventually became a must-stop for many Japanese tourists throughout the years. At times tour buses would pull up with loads of Japanese customers. When the exchange rate was favorable, there were times that we literally had to limit the amount of guitars these customers could purchase. I wanted to make sure we had enough quality stock for our next visitors.

When I first opened, I was selling pre-CBS Stratocasters for well under $1,000. Americans themselves were asleep, but the well informed Japanese buyers recognized opportunity.

It can be cyclical. I ended up repurchasing many guitars that I sold to Japanese buyers over the years, for which they made nice profits. I was happy to have the instruments back on our shores.

———

The market is constantly evolving. At one time, beautiful dot neck ES-335s from 1959 went for $1,800, which seemed like a lot of money.

Shortly thereafter, these guitars became the model of choice to Lee Ritenour, Larry Carlton, Jay Graydon, and many other top studio musicians. The prices quickly escalated, and about three months after I sold a beautiful 1959 for $1,800, I purchased a lesser example for $3,000. What else could I do?

It was an opportunity to make money, and I had to bite the bullet. I had to pay $3,000 for a guitar that I could easily sell for $4,000. That's just the nature of the business. You have to go with the flow and pay legitimate and timely prices for guitars that can easily be resold for more.

Prior to 2008, there really was no time that values had declined across the board. But 2008 was a wake-up call, and many values were realigned. Don't forget, real estate, antiques, and everything was hit pretty hard. Since then, however, values have begun to go up again at a rapid pace.

Recently I had the opportunity to buy back part of a big collection of guitars that I sold about twenty-five years ago. These guitars were super high end and primarily acoustic. Some were fantastic examples of early Martin flat-tops. Many of the models were Brazilian Rosewood style 28s to 45s. I paid many times what I had previously sold them for but was happy to buy them back, knowing that it was unlikely that I'd lose money on them.

Many people might feel funny about paying so much more for instruments they already owned, but I look at it as a new and fresh opportunity each time. I love having them back in the store, even if only temporarily.

———

In the end, we're all just custodians of these things. I believe fine vintage guitars will outlive many generations, and will be sold and resold throughout every corner of the globe. It has to do with their classic beauty and functionality of design, as well as utility. Functional art that's made to be played.

———

I just received a phone call letting me know that my old friend Bob Turner just passed away in September 2015. Bob was a pioneer in the vintage guitar business, and he will be greatly missed. He was truly one of the most unforgettable characters I have ever met.

14

KING OF
THE SWAPS

G uitar-playing collectors are often eccentric human beings, may-be because you have to be an obsessive to master music. That same obsession might drive you to acquire and hold onto more and more instruments as the years go on. Each instrument does something else. Each has its own tone and feel.

I don't really know why people do these things. I do know that over the years, I've become well versed in dealing with such people. Sometimes you have to just hang out and be patient to win the ever-elusive "gold."

Back in the seventies, there was always loads of stuff at the Saugus swap meet outside of Los Angeles.

This was back in the era when swap meets were really good, before the dealers took over. They were composed almost entirely of private parties bringing to market high-quality goods. Hard as it might be to believe, the only other outlets to sell were the newspapers or individual garage sales.

I used to get up every Sunday at 4:00 a.m. to make the rounds from swap meet to swap meet. I'd be there so early that I had to bring a flashlight to see what goods were being set up! I would practically sprint from person to person as they were unloading their goods off their trucks or cars.

Martin 1928 0-45. (Photos by Jen Angkahan)

Looking back, it's incredible how much great gear I acquired that way. Living in LA, it was a common occurrence to see old Fenders. Every Sunday I'd see people unloading blond Fender two-piece amps and plenty of tweed cases. I came to realize that those Gibson brown cases almost always contained something special. To many people, these were just old guitars and amps that needed fixing that they wanted to unload. Their value was undocumented, and unknown.

It really was a smorgasbord out there. Often I'd purchase other vintage stuff such as radios, antiques, old suitcases, and the like.

Okay, so maybe I'm one of those obsessives . . .

Over time, all of us regulars became pretty familiar with each other. There was this one old-timer who had been swap-meetin' from the beginning. He was a tall, good-looking, rangy old cowboy named Don Weston. He must've been in his late sixties when I met him, and he used to talk about his experiences as a singing cowboy in movies, and in particular, being Gene Autry's guitar teacher. This is now pretty much a bygone era of our culture, but the B movie cycles of singing cowboys churned out in volume by Monogram and Republic studios in the forties was a boon to musicians of that ilk. Gene Autry was the king of that world—probably because he invested his earnings as a singing cowboy into TV and radio stations and made a fortune, eventually owning the professional baseball team the California (now Los Angeles) Angels.

Don was one of those journeyman players who backed up Gene, Roy Rogers, Merle Travis, and all the big cowboy stars. A few of his tunes even made it on the Billboard charts in the forties. Of course, by the seventies that world had pretty much evaporated, but he still had a twinkle in his eye when he spoke about it.

Don always had a few guitars displayed, but it seemed to me he was buying more than selling. The guitars he brought to sell were generally no better than average, but I asked if he had more and he said the good stuff was still at home.

"When do I get to see that?" I said.

Don strung me along for a while, then one Sunday he gave me his address in North Hollywood. On the agreed-upon day, I showed up and he showed me a treasure trove of vintage guitars! Old Strats, ES-335s, Gibson archtops, Martin flat-tops, Gretsch 6120s, and hundreds of quality ukuleles, as well as a few banjos and mandolins. He had excellent taste and really knew what was good.

Then Don casually pulled out a brown case, unsnapped the latch, and inside was an unbelievably clean Gibson 1940 Rosewood J-200—a once-in-a-lifetime guitar.

The guitars he amassed over the years were truly amazing, and most were very clean and original. I was practically foaming at the mouth. I tried to keep a poker face, but Don could see right through me. This wasn't his first time at the rodeo.

I tried to negotiate, but he kept changing the subject, talking about shotguns or old-time saddle makers. He wouldn't let me get to first base. In retrospect, I think he most enjoyed the fact that I was dying to buy them. It wasn't a price thing. He just liked tormenting me. He was a true collector and couldn't bear to part with any of them.

This went on for years. Occasionally he'd sell me some of his more mediocre guitars but wouldn't let go of the good ones. Being relentless, and not shy about what I wanted, I would call Don approximately every couple months asking, "Have you considered selling me any of your stuff yet?"

"Not at this time," was always the answer. Don was very polite about it. I couldn't even get him to quote me a high price, which I probably would have been willing to pay. He knew I had a lot of high-quality guitars, and I think it might have been a competitive thing. We were friendly, but the old rustler viewed it as a contest. He liked me, but he viewed me as Johnny-come-lately. He got off on teasing me.

I remained in contact with Don for probably fifteen years, always asking the same question and getting the same answer. Sadly, after Don passed away, I would occasionally call his wife to ask how she was doing. She knew I really wanted to buy Don's instruments but she had been so in love with him, she couldn't get herself to sell them either. I had all but given up on acquiring Don's things. It was the killer collection that got away.

Some years went by. I went about my business and stopped calling Don's wife. Then, one day the phone rang, and it was Don's son on the line. He told me his mom had passed away and before she died, she had instructed him to call me.

It is sad when someone dies and you delve into their collection. It's a personal glimpse into an individual's obsessions, private moments,

Gibson 1940 Rosewood J-200. (Photos by Jen Angkahan)

hopes, and dreams. We all save stuff, never considering that we won't take it with us off this earth. All the things that define a true collector during his lifetime are at the core of his identity, but when he's gone they rarely have the same meaning for the people left to deal with them. Sometimes the survivors don't even understand the things that were collected. Some people are just hoarders, and they save a lot of junk, which gets tossed out.

I guess the same will happen to me someday, but there won't be any mystery about why I collected all these instruments—I was, and always am, in pursuit of the best.

I was sad about Don's wife passing away, but I could hardly contain myself by the prospect of buying all those amazing guitars. Don's son asked if I could come right over because he wanted me to see the extent of the collection and see if we could make a deal. A rocket ship couldn't have gotten me over there faster!

When I got there, I discovered that the collection was a lot more massive than I originally thought. This dude collected a variety of stuff, not just guitars.

There were early Washburn presentation model guitars, an early Ditson guitar made by Martin, lots of Martin guitars of all sizes from early New York models, to literally hundreds of ukuleles of all descriptions, including dozens of Koa Martin ukes from the thirties. This was before the recent ukulele boom, and there was not a lot of interest in them at the time. Yes, Don had been a very active collector for decades.

I went through everything and bought every music-related item that was quality, which was considerable. Don was very finicky in his tastes. Finally, we were down to the last numbers, and his son threw in his collection of straight-edged razors, which all had ornate, hand-carved ivory or silver handles, and we had a deal. I should've bought his extensive gun collection, but I didn't really know anything about them and still don't.

Luckily, I had been saving and had money at the time, but I knew I would have to tell Don's son I could give him almost all of the money immediately and the rest in a postdated check, giving me some time to sell some of the instruments to make good on my commitment. I had to wholesale a number of instruments to cover my debt quickly. After a couple of weeks, I accumulated enough money to cover the postdated check. Even though this was the mid-eighties and instruments were only bringing a fraction of today's prices, it still amounted to a lot of bread. Don's son was well aware of the market values at the time but also knew it was advantageous to sell so many instruments at once. When the smoke cleared, it was by far the biggest and best deal I had ever made.

And I had that once-in-a-lifetime Rosewood J-200.

I have a friend named Andy Roth who was living in LA at the time but has since moved to Hawaii. He was very much into ukes, and I sold them to him by the box load at prices that today would seem unbelievably cheap. There were loads of Martins, Gibsons, and Gretschs, as well as Nunes, Kamakas, and other Hawaiian ukes. There were National and other resonator ukes, pineapple ukes, and one uke that was given to Mickey Rooney by the mayor of Honolulu. I practically sold them by the pound. I wasn't that much into them and liquidated them accordingly.

A childhood friend of mine named Richard Glick purchased my Ditson presentation model guitar, which was by far the fanciest parlor

Martin uke. (Photo by Jen Angkahan)

guitar I have ever seen. Along with massive and intricate pearl inlays, there was also silver inlaid on the gorgeous pattern on the fingerboard.

I sold a lot of instruments at the time that I now regret, including Gibson L-5s, Stratocasters, the Ditson, and some great Gretsch instruments, but it's important to keep your cash flowing to stay in business. I guess I have to keep in mind that at the time I sold them the prices were fair, but it seems like nothing compared with today's prices. Like all business dealings from real estate, to stocks, to automobiles, everything is in the timing.

You might ask what happened to that Rosewood J-200. Like so many wonderful guitars in my collection, I sold that to a good friend and collector who shall remain nameless. I immediately regretted doing this. I attempted to buy it back for many, many years. I am nothing if not persistent. Finally, after twenty years, he let me have it. A couple weeks later, he called me up and told me he couldn't live without it . . . So, the beat goes on.

I understand his predicament entirely. I just have to keep on reminding myself, "You can't take it with you." Don Weston taught me that lesson. So, upon my death, when my family finds all those old-school straight razors, now they'll know I wasn't too crazy. I have them for a reason . . .

15

THE ELUSIVE
'BURST

The 1958–60 Sunburst Les Paul has achieved hallowed status in the world of guitar collecting. I believe that specific model did nothing less than create the vintage guitar market. It has defined the market, and defied all its naysayers. It is one of the instruments that have consistently appreciated over time. It is one of the most coveted models by all guitar enthusiasts.

Back in the day, when we all first started looking for them, they were a whopping $800! Forty years later, a super-flamy clean original can easily fetch up to a half-million bucks. What is it about this guitar?

It begins with Mike Bloomfield, one of the most influential guitarists in history. The story goes that Mike heard Eric Clapton's Marshall-driven 'Burst tone on the John Mayall's *Blues Breakers* record, and he had to get one himself. Though almost forgotten today, through his work with Dylan and Paul Butterfield, Mike was the hottest blues rock player on the planet for a brief few years. After he was seen and heard playing his 'Burst, it whet the appetite of everyone, including many players across the pond in England, like Jimmy Page. And so its legend spread.

Designwise, the 'Burst represented the apogee of Les Paul's lifelong experiment with solidbody guitars. It had evolved through crude trapeze tailpieces, goldtops, and P-90 pickups. By late 1957, Les Paul Standards sported the famed tune-o-matic bridge, stud tailpiece, and the brand new Patent Applied For (P.A.F.) humbucking pickups, designed by Seth Lover. All you need to do is compare Freddie King's original "Hideaway" on a P-90-equipped goldtop with Clapton's cover on the *Blues Breakers* to hear the difference. Freddie's tone was killer in a different way, but those P-90s could not get that thick, meaty tone of those P.A.F.s.

The thing that most distinguished it was the tops. You could hide three mismatched pieces of wood under gold paint, but the sunbursts had transparent tops. That meant that each guitar had its own distinct fingerprint—some were heavily flamed, some were thick-flamed, some were thin-flamed, and some were chevrons, set on an angle. Each one had unique beauty, as well as musical utility.

Then, fittingly, after a couple years, they "flamed out." They weren't modern enough. They hardly sold. By 1961, they were discontinued, morphed into the SG shape, and Les's relationship with Gibson was over. All in, there were probably seventeen to eighteen hundred 1958–60 Les Paul Standards produced. That's it.

But their mystique would only grow over time.

―――――

In the early seventies, my standard guitar search M.O. was cold-calling members of Local 47, the LA Musician's Union. This proved to be very lucrative, but for years I was never able to dig up a Sunburst Les Paul through the Union handbook.

I remember this one particular day, I had made it through all the *A*'s in the book, and I was working my way through the *B*s. I contacted a man name Mel "Nat" Brown. Brown had the nickname Nat because he was a disciple of Nat King Cole and did a number of Cole's tunes in his repertoire. I asked if he had any older Gibson, Fender, or Martin guitars that he was willing to part with. He said he had a guitar that he

Norman holding a 1959 Gibson Les Paul Sunburst Standard. (Photo by Marlene Harris)

wasn't using much and that it was a Gibson solidbody. I did not want to get my hopes up because I had been disappointed so many times in my search for the holy grail. Brown couldn't give me much more detailed information because he didn't use the guitar that often, but he knew it was "red." I asked if it was a Sunburst, but all he could recall was that it was red. I kept inquiring about details but got nowhere. He told me that he had a gig at the top of the Holiday Inn in Hollywood and said he would be happy to bring it that night. I figured it had to be an SG, because there were so many red ones.

Marlene and I went to Brown's gig that night, and I vividly remember going up in the elevator to the top floor. When the door opened, there was a lattice screen directly in front of us. I heard Nat playing a cover of Johnny Nash's "I Can See Clearly Now." I could see through the screen and there it was, a Sunburst Les Paul Standard! Talk about seeing clearly!

The adrenaline was pumping full bore. I couldn't wait to get in and talk to him about the guitar. Nat wanted $1,500 for it, and I was happy to give it to him without negotiating. I believe at the time they were bringing about $2,500 retail, but everybody wanted to own one.

I had gotten my first one.

Another time I was visiting my mom in Hallandale, Florida. Hallandale is on the ocean in between North Miami Beach and Fort Lauderdale. I would do my usual routine. Immediately after getting off the plane, I would get the newspaper (the *Miami Herald*) to see if there were any guitars for sale in the classifieds, then make the rounds I used to make when I lived in Miami. I went to all the pawnshops and music stores, hoping to find something vintage and cool. I went into ACE Music, which was the biggest store in Miami at the time, and asked one of the salespeople if they had any older Gibson, Fender, or Martin guitars. I said I was a dealer now living in California and that I was willing to pay some high prices for vintage guitars. The salesperson showed me a couple older guitars. One was a Larson Brothers Maurer acoustic from the thirties and the other a blue Melody Maker (SG type).

I purchased both guitars and as I was loading the guitars in my trunk, a raggedy-looking fellow came up to me and asked if I was looking for more guitars. He had heard me ask the salesperson for vintage guitars, and he watched as I bought two. I said, "Sure, what do you have?"

He said, "I have an older Les Paul model guitar." Yes, I was definitely interested, I told him, and I would pay good money for it if it was nice. He said, "It's nice, but it also happens to be left-handed." I asked him some questions about the guitar and damn if it didn't sound like a Sunburst Standard.

Through the years, I can't tell you how many people have told me they have a 1950s Sunburst Les Paul and it turned out to be bullshit. It got to the point where I almost didn't take people seriously when they brought it up. They were so damn elusive that I wasn't going to get my hopes up.

I was staying in my mom's high-rise apartment building in Hallandale. Most of the building was leased to yearly tenants, but there was

Gibson 1960 Les Paul Sunburst left-handed. (Photo by Norman Harris)

one section that was used as daily hotel rentals. I told the man where I was staying and my room number. I said, "If you want to sell the guitar, be at my room at 10:00 a.m." I really didn't figure I would ever see him again, so I set up the appointment early to make sure it didn't kill my whole day.

I actually forgot about the appointment because I didn't think he was for real. I was getting dressed when the doorbell rang. The door had a peephole and, as I looked through to see who it was, I could see he was holding . . . yes, a lefty Sunburst Les Paul! I opened the door and let the man in. I was able to deduce that the guitar was a 1960 model. It had a cherry sunburst vibrant finish and was in excellent condition. The man was holding the guitar. He didn't have a case. We negotiated, and I bought it for $2,500.

You never know which seemingly crazy person might actually show up with the goods! I'm glad I didn't just blow the man off.

I sold that guitar to someone else pretty soon after I bought it. The truth is, these guitars change hands quite often because their value has become astronomical. Back then, though, it was kind of like a stock that kept on going up. You never knew when it would hit the ceiling. People bellyached when they were $2,500, and again when they were $5,000. By the time they reached $8,500, I had about fourteen of them in my collection. I regret to say this, but I got "cold feet," and sold a bunch of them off! If only I'd held on . . .

"If only . . ." That's the guitar collector's mantra.

I know that Paul McCartney has a left-handed 1960 Les Paul Standard. I often wonder if the Les Paul I purchased that day may now be in the very capable hands of Paul McCartney. There can't be too many of them, so I would say it's definitely possible.

16

ADVERTISING
PAYS

My advertisements in the *LA Times* always seemed to pay off
nicely. Looking back, I find it amazing just how many wonderful guitars came to me through those ads.

Once I received a call from a man who said he had a very clean, older Fender Stratocaster with a sunburst finish, in "excellent" condition.
When I asked him what color the case was, he told me "brown," and I
had to conceal my excitement. A brown case can mean many things,

Fender 1962 Stratocaster. (Photo by Jen Angkahan)

but it usually means we're talking early-sixties vintage. I could not wait to get directions and make it over to his house. I got in my car and sped as fast as I could to the Long Beach area.

When I got there, the man introduced himself as Bob and pulled out the Strat case. He wasn't kidding. It was super-clean. He popped it open, revealing a stunning slab board Sunburst Stratocaster. Clearly, it had been hardly played, which would put it in the "excellent" condition column in my book. Then he also pulled out a gorgeous brown Fender Concert amp, which was also hardly used. Did I want it? Of course I wanted it.

Then he asked me if I was interested in John D'Angelico guitars. I said absolutely. I tried to keep it cool as I asked him about that guitar.

For those of you who might not be familiar with the name, John D'Angelico was known as the greatest archtop maker of his time. His original designs had been influenced by Gibson, but he ended up build-

D'Angelico 1942 custom Bob. (Photos by Jen Angkahan)

ing his own "Excels" and "New Yorkers," which were beautiful art-deco beasts in the forties and fifties, during the heyday of jazz guitar. Almost all of the most well-known players had a "D.A." Being able to afford one was a sign that you had arrived.

Bob told me D'Angelico was his uncle, and that "Uncle John" had given him a guitar for his thirteenth birthday. Bob reached into his closet and pulled out an early pebble grained seventeen-inch archtop case. When he pulled out the guitar, I saw that it was a gorgeous blond non-cutaway Excel model. The wood on the back was spectacular and flamed to death. He also pointed at the inlay on the top of the headstock. It was heart-shaped with the name *Bob* inlaid in the middle of the heart! This was an intimate and personal statement by the master, and I knew immediately I'd never see one like it again and that I had to have it.

I negotiated the best deal I could. I was determined to leave with both guitars and the amp. Bob was aware of the value of them but said he could use the money to do some remodeling of his house. He said he hadn't played guitar in years and felt this would give him enough money to do what he had to around the house. I bought them all and couldn't wait to get home to play them. Even to this day, I still have both the guitars and the Concert amp, priceless pieces in my collection.

The bottom line is, my "Top Dollar Paid" ad was a signal to sellers that I knew the value of rare and special guitars. In the early eighties, most local stores wouldn't know what a D'Angelico even was. Most local stores at the time dealt in new guitars and wouldn't have even known what was fair market value for a 1962 slab board Strat. But now, thanks to the wonders of the Internet, everybody knows or thinks they know . . .

=====

Another call that came in was an older lady who said she had her late sister's Martin guitar. Her sister had passed away and left her the Martin. She told me she knew nothing about it, but she believed it was probably from the sixties. Over the phone, I coaxed her to get the guitar and look up at the heel block inside the body to read me the model and serial number. Unfortunately, her eyesight had been failing and she couldn't get enough light in the guitar to make out what was stamped inside. All right, so no information available there.

Then she told me she felt the guitar was worth about $1,200. I asked her how she came up with that number, and she informed me that she had taken it to a local store and that's what they told her. They said they did not purchase used guitars but that was their guess as to the value.

Judging from her description of the condition of the guitar, I could tell that it was clean, but I wasn't excited because without the information on the neck block, it was inconclusive. Also, the fact that a music store had already evaluated it, I felt it could have been from the early seventies. She lived down in Orange County by Knotts Berry farm, which was a schlep for me, and traffic was always a bear. So I made an appointment to see the guitar a couple days later. If I had thought it might be anything special, I would have immediately jumped in my car and drove to her house.

A couple days later, I arrived to see the guitar, and she pulled out the case. It was a much older case than I had anticipated. I had seen lots of guitars in cases that were much older so that didn't mean anything.

When I popped open the case, I saw a beautiful D-28. I saw that the guitar had a tortoise pickguard and herringbone trim. I saw that it had bar frets, which would've predated it to 1934 or 1935. Then I looked at the heel block for the serial number and discovered it was a 1934! This was the first year of production for D-28s. The guitar was in remarkable condition. I didn't want to get too worked up because in the past I had blown a few deals by acting too excited. I gave the lady her asking price, and I figured I would write down her mailing address and send her an additional check after I got home. I wanted to be fair, but I didn't want to blow the deal by telling her the guitar was worth much more.

There had been a couple of instances when I told the seller that their guitar was worth much more and they decided if it's worth that much maybe they would not sell it. So I had learned from my mistakes. At the time, the guitar was worth between $10,000 and $12,000. I mailed her a check for an additional sum, and I almost immediately sold the guitar for $12,000.

You don't want to know how much that guitar is worth today. Of course, with hindsight, I wish I had kept it, but at the time, I made an outstanding profit. Sometimes the businessman supersedes the collector in me. I'm sure that if the local music store she went to made her any kind of offer, they could have purchased the guitar for much less. It's amazing to me that a store wouldn't at least do a little research and see what they were passing on.

———

I regret to say that stumbling across a rare bird like that is increasingly unlikely in this modern age. It really was "the Wild West" back then. The newspapers were a prime source for classified ads. There was a lot of promotion for their classified section, and people waited with great anticipation for the newspapers to come out, especially the Sunday editions. The Sunday editions were generally many times larger than the weekly classified ads. Garage and estate sales were plentiful and it was a great outlet for people to sell their things. There were also publications such as the *Penny Saver, Nifty Nickel, White Sheet*, and eventually the *Recycler*, solely dedicated to classified ads.

I already told you how I used to follow the trucks coming out of the *LA Times* in order to catch the first drop off of the newspapers. I discovered that the *Sunday LA Times* always appeared on Saturdays. Of course it was Saturday's news, but with Sunday's classifieds. I would get the papers, mark the ads that I was interested in, and start making calls on a pay phone. (Remember those?) Sometimes people were pretty upset that I was calling so early, so I'd have to lie and say I was going to work, but that I had cash on me and would like to come by and pick up the guitar before work. If the ad was really special, I would sometimes recruit Marlene to wait for a little while and then call about the ad, pretending she was a different potential buyer. This was before call waiting, so I wanted to tie up those telephone lines so no one else could call.

Marlene would start asking a lot of rudimentary questions, like how many strings the guitar had, what color it was, and other dull, ignorant things, just to keep the conversation going and tie up the line. She also would ask why they were selling the guitar, how long they had the guitar, et cetera. They would generally say, "There is a guy coming over to look at the guitar" but she would continue asking questions. She'd really drag it out and was expert at doing this.

At the very end of their conversation, she would say, "I'm sorry, but this is not what I was interested in!" By this time hopefully I was pulling into their driveway. Eventually, after answering a lot of stupid questions and being hassled, they were glad to sell their guitar to me, so they wouldn't have to deal with it anymore and be bothered by answering anyone else's stupid questions!

Eventually I searched out someone working at the *LA Times* and gave them a kickback if they helped me by giving me information about the ads before they came out. I did whatever it took to land the big score. When I was younger, I played a lot of sports, which taught me strategy. Strategy can be trickery or deception. I definitely am not telling anyone to break the law, but slightly bending the rules can be very profitable.

━━━━━

In the early eighties, the *Recycler* became a game changer overnight. It would come out Thursday mornings around 7:00 a.m. The main office was in Sherman Oaks, about seven miles from my house. On Thursday mornings, I would go down to the *Recycler* office, coffee in hand, and buy every edition—the Valley, Los Angeles, San Gabriel, and even Palms Springs and Orange County. I would start with the editions close by and would work my way through all of them no matter how far away.

Eventually a lot of people began using the *Recycler* to buy stuff and the lines at 7:00 a.m. starting going around the block. There were people looking to buy cars, antiques, houses, sporting goods, and everything else under the sun. After a while, there were other people looking to buy guitars in line with me at the *Recycler*, and the competition became quite fierce. When folks become aware that something is profitable, competition arises. I remember one guy was only interested in Marshall amps. We were not going for the same things, and so we generally stayed out of each other's way.

When looking through the ads, you had to move quickly. I would earmark the ads that were most important and make my calls according to priority. Sometimes if the locations were far away, I had to ask the seller to give me his word that he would hold his goods until I arrived. I would say, "Give me until 9:00 a.m., please," just to give me a chance to get there. I would assure the seller that I was serious and coming with cash.

This went on for quite a few years, and it seemed like each week there were more people waiting in line. Even though the competition was strong, it was very exciting. It always felt like I was prospecting.

You never knew what treasure you might dig up. One thing I learned was always to ask if they had anything else they wanted to sell. Sometimes the thing I primarily came for was nothing compared to something else I found there. Sometimes the seller needed to be persuaded to sell other guitars. I always came with cash in hand just in case there were more things that became available. Some of my best acquisitions were secondary ones.

———

I never put a time limit on how long I was willing to work. This certainly was not just a 9-to-5 job. If I got a call back from San Diego and it was midnight, I got in my car and went on my way. Eventually things changed with Craigslist, eBay, and all the other Internet sources. Even the *LA Times* and the *Recycler* began posting online classifieds. These ads posted immediately so people didn't have to stand in line waiting to purchase their newspaper editions. I truly believe that if these newspapers delayed posting ads until, let's say, Thursday, people would once again wait anxiously to buy goods.

If you look at the *Times* classifieds these days, it is mainly dealer ads. The classified section is now so small, it is only a fraction of the size it once was. There are very few private-party ads. There is no need to buy the publications if ads are already posted online. I think newspaper sales would improve if the ads were only released on a certain day. Even the *Recycler* to this day is a much smaller publication, with much fewer ads. Posting their ads online does not build up demand like they once had. Even if the papers gave private parties free ads in order to build up these classified sections, I believe it would give more folks a reason to buy their publications. But the newspaper business isn't a growth industry anymore, and that's depressing to me.

17

WORLD FAMOUS TINKERER

G uitar players are often chronic tinkerers. It could have something to do with that ever-elusive search for the "right" sound. Or maybe it's more of an obsessive need to remanufacture such sounds from the guitar you just happen to have in your possession.

I can't tell you how many guitars I've encountered that were fucked with, almost beyond redemption—I've seen it all: shaved necks, terrible refins, homemade crack repairs, changed pickups, tuners, tailpieces, the list goes on and on.

Even at the beginning of my journey in the vintage guitar world, I was a stickler for originality. I knew then, as I know now, that most collectors will not pay top dollar for "player-grade instruments." I've made it my business always to look under the hood. Especially, if you're dealing with a 1958–60 Les Paul—any funny business with the solders on those P.A.F.s can cost you thousands. I pride myself on knowing what's original and being straightforward to my customers, in all aspects. But occasionally, I've second-guessed myself.

———

I was on the fence about telling this story, but it's pretty amusing. Back in the late seventies, a lot of local guitarists found their way to my store. It became somewhat of a hangout. One of these fellows was a very nice, young man who seemed like a regular guy. He'd often come in with a six-pack of beer, and share it with everyone in the store. It didn't matter what time of day it was, we all enjoyed cracking a cold one and talking music and guitars.

Like all of us, he dreamed of owning an original Sunburst Les Paul.

He was an excellent player, and I had no doubt he would succeed. After getting a substantial signing bonus from a major record label, he came to me, ready to do business. He chose two Les Pauls from my collection, and we made a deal. One had a moderately flamed top, and I believe the tuners were replaced. The other Les Paul had the flame top of doom. It was in excellent condition with kind of a honey-burst finish. It was radically flamed and fully original.

He paid $5,500 for the moderately flamed one, and $6,500 for the one with the killer top. The prices at the time were a little under market value, but I liked the kid, knew he had talent, and wanted to give him a good deal. Even though he has never been known for playing Les Pauls, he has been pictured with these guitars on occasion over the years.

After that purchase, he came in from time to time and bought a few other guitars from us. I remember one was an excellent Don Musser flat-top guitar, a wonderful sounding instrument.

As expected, he ended up having tremendous success with his career and later was anointed with "Guitar God" status. However, the days of him hanging out in the shop and sharing his sixer were long gone. As the years went on, I never saw or heard from him. Granted, he was busy, touring the world with his band.

Decades later, in early 2003, I received a call from him. I was sincerely happy to hear from him. Before we could get through any small talk, he cut to the chase.

"Norm," he said. "You remember the two Les Pauls I bought from you, years ago."

"I'd never forget them," I said.

"Well, on one of the Les Pauls, the pickups aren't P.A.F.s."

"That's strange," I said. "Because the first thing I do whenever buying a Sunburst Les Paul is open up the pickups to make sure they are, in fact, P.A.F.s."

As I've already said, I always try to be very accurate in describing guitars, and checking those pickups would be the first order of business. I could not imagine ever buying or selling a Sunburst Les Paul without doing my due diligence. Of course this was twenty years after the sale, so I didn't necessarily have the actual memory of checking those specific guitars in my gray matter.

In any business, the customer is "always right," even if he's wrong. So I figured I'd compromise.

"I'll be glad to give you a refund or even buy back the guitar for four or five times what you paid, because the prices have gone up so much.

Gibson Les Paul, no pickups. (Photo courtesy of Norman Harris)

You should come over here and give me a kiss for selling you those guitars. This is probably the best investment you ever made!"

He said, "What would the guitar be worth if it was completely untampered with?"

I said, "A lot." And I meant it.

He said, "Then I want you to pay me the difference, because I thought this guitar had original pickups."

"Are you kidding?" I said. "I sold those guitars to you twenty years ago. How do I know that you or one of your techs didn't change out the pickups?"

He had been well known for modifying and custom building his own guitars, so that was a red flag. He also definitely seemed kind of agitated, and I had known he had substance abuse problems, which didn't make me trust him any more in this situation.

I tried to cut through the crap. "What do you want from me?"

"I already told you, Norm. The difference between what the guitar was worth with changed pickups, as opposed to having the pickups being original."

So I offered to find him a set of P.A.F.s, or to buy the guitar back for five times what he paid. He was trying to stick me with a raw deal, but at least there would be an added memorabilia value in addition to the normal worth of the instrument, even with the P.A.F.s gone. He said he'd get back to me.

I never heard back from him, and I often wondered, "Could I possibly have overlooked opening the guitar's pickups to check for authenticity?" It was highly unlikely, but it still ate at me a little.

========

A few years later, one of my customers came into the store bearing pictures of some of the Nudie Suits he had been recently buying and selling. (Nudie was the legendary western tailor who made fancy cus-tom-made suits for famous Western stars.) Along with the pictures of the suits, he showed me pictures he had taken of popular LA bands of the time. As I browsed through the photos, I took some satisfaction in knowing that many of these people were customers of mine.

Then I stopped short. There was a photo of this particular "Guitar God." It literally took my breath away. Why? Because it showed him playing the exact Les Paul that was in question with the neck pickup *completely removed* from the guitar! You could tell by the picture that this was taken a long time ago because he was still a very young man.

I said to my friend, "How much do you want for this photo?" He didn't want to sell it. "I'll give you $250 for it."

"Sold!"

This picture was the absolute proof I needed that he had in fact modified the guitar by removing the pickup. It confirmed that I did do my due diligence, and he was just trying to hustle me at that moment. After acquiring the photograph, I showed it to some of my friends, and they said that there are a lot of shots of him playing this guitar with the pickup removed. I felt stupid for paying $250 for the picture, but at the time I felt this was my only proof, in case he ever showed up again try-ing to get over on me.

If he had been playing the guitar with any two other after-market pickups in the guitar, I would not be able to prove my case. However, the empty cavity totally confirmed that he had modified the Les Paul. To this day he never manned up and apologized to me for his accusa-tion. I don't hold it against him because maybe this was at a bad time in his life, but I still wouldn't mind receiving an apology!

18

THE ONES THAT
GOT AWAY

I'm known around this business as a man willing to put his money
where his mouth is. Believe it or not, I actually tend to be somewhat
conservative. Often I have had opportunities to buy instruments that at
the time seemed like all the money in the world. In almost every case I
ended up regretting not purchasing the instrument, because the overall
escalation in prices has been so dramatic, and instruments that originally seemed to be so expensive turned out to be dirt cheap.

In 1968 and 1969, late-1950s Sunburst Les Paul Standards were going for around $800. I know this seems impossible, but remember that
they were only ten years old at the time! It seemed like so much money, and accounting for inflation, $800 was equal to about $5,200 today,
which is still pretty damn cheap, considering. I remember passing on a
few, and it was agonizing. Dot neck ES-335s were going for about $300.
Blackguard Telecasters and 1950s maple neck Stratocasters were going for $300–$400. I even remember a time in my first store when I had
about six pre-CBS Strats on the wall. This was in 1975, and you could
have had your choice for $750.

I was playing in my band Katmandu in 1969, and a friend of mine,
Jeff Wityak, who now lives in California, called me to say he had a line
on a Sunburst Les Paul. An old fireman who lived near his house in
South Miami owned it. I went over to Jeff's place, and we both drove to

see this old man just a few miles away. I can still remember going into his house and watching the man pull out a brown Gibson cardboard soft case. Inside the case was one of the cleanest, flamiest 'Bursts ever. The flames were extremely wide and were on a chevron. This 'Burst was completely out of control. I really didn't know what I was looking at, but I wanted this guitar in the worst way. I can still see the guitar in my mind.

I asked the old-timer how much he wanted and he said $1,500. This was twice what any of these would have gone for at the time. I tried my best to negotiate, but he was a stubborn son of a bitch. He would not lower his price a dime. I think he enjoyed teasing us with it, and he knew I really wanted it. But I wouldn't budge, either. I had enough money but could not see myself paying twice the guitar's value.

For a few years we kept contacting the man, hoping he would re-consider. This was just not going to happen. One day we called and his phone number had been disconnected. We went to his house and he no longer lived there. I'm sure he passed away long ago, and somewhere that guitar still exists. To this day, I dream about that guitar.

Another guitar that I remember about the same time, also in Miami, was an early Gibson Byrdland. This was not like any Byrdland I have ever seen. It was in factory-black finish with a headstock similar to an F-5 mandolin, with the curlicue and a flowerpot. Once again I asked this man how much he wanted, and he said $1,500. This seemed like so much money. I tried to negotiate but was unable to make it happen. Somewhere in South Florida, this guitar still exists. I know that some-day I'll see it again.

Unfortunately there are too many of these stories. Sometimes people take pleasure in torturing would-be buyers. In retrospect if I only stepped up, I would've had them, but my conservative nature took over, and I was unwilling to speculate and pay over market value. These gui-

Gibson Les Paul. (Photo courtesy of Norman Harris)

tars seemed so overpriced at the time, but I just could not pull the trigger and these regrets I will have forever.

In LA, through my relentless cold-calling folks in the Musician's Union roster, I found a man named Stanley "Curly" Clements. I bought several instruments from him. One axe I didn't buy was a 1930s Martin Herringbone D-28 with a Bigsby neck. I was such a stickler for originality, I felt the Bigsby neck was a modification and a sacrilege. I just didn't see the value in such an instrument, because I didn't understand the importance of Paul Bigsby's history in the electric guitar world, as well as its impossible rarity. Through the years I owned a couple of Bigsby guitars and steels, but I passed on quite a few others. By the time I realized what I didn't buy, it was gone.

Another instrument I was not aware of at the time was a beautiful prewar Gibson Advanced Jumbo, which was Gibson's rosewood answer to the Martin D-28. Some time in the mid-seventies, this guitar was

131

offered to me at $2,500. I just did not realize the rarity of what I was looking at. I countered at $1,500 for the guitar, which seemed high at the time. Once again I missed the boat and could not see into the future. Another costly mistake, but who knew?

A number of years later, a friend offered me two late-1950s Les Paul Standards. One was a terrifying flamy Sunburst Les Paul, and the other was a late-1950s Goldtop with P.A.F.s that had a floral pickguard like an ES-295. Both guitars were totally mint. I knew these guitars were unbelievably rare, but I just could not get with the price. If only I had a little more foresight . . . If only . . .

Sometimes you get a slew of great guitars and miss just one special instrument. Because I was one of the only stores in Los Angeles to specialize in vintage instruments, from time to time I would receive a call from someone selling their guitar or their guitar collection. I almost had a monopoly at the time for buying vintage guitars in Los Angeles.

Other stores would refer sellers to me, and more than often, I gave them a kickback or a fee for sending people my way.

My old friend and bandmate from the Angel City Rhythm Band, Dan Duehren, was working with me at the time. We received a call from a gentleman in the Santa Barbara area who had some guitars to sell. He told me about a few instruments he had, including several old Fenders. One was a sunburst stacked-knob Jazz Bass. There were a couple of Sunburst Stratocasters and there were a few other Fenders—a custom-color Jazzmaster (Lake Placid blue), a candy-apple red Jaguar, and a Sunburst Fender electric twelve-string. He said he had a few more things and would show me if I came over. He said he used to work for Fender and at one time had his own store. Danny had a pickup truck, so we got directions and couldn't hit the road fast enough.

When we arrived we were blown away. He had what he said, but he also had about thirty more instruments. There was an early 1960s L-5

CES Sunburst, dot neck ES-335, a blond 1950s Fender electric mandolin, a J-200, and many more, including some vintage Fender amps.
Almost everything was fully original and in remarkable condition. We
spent a few hours assessing the guitars and then went into negotiation.
Once again he knew what he had, but he was happy to be able to sell
so many instruments at once. This was around 1980, so even though
it seemed expensive at the time, by today's standards it was a bargain.

After we consummated the deal, we wrote a check and loaded the
instruments in Danny's truck. Just before leaving the gentleman pulled
out one more bass. He said this was his main instrument and he was
not ready to let it go. He wanted me to see it in case he decided to sell it
at a later time. It was in a tweed case, and when he opened it up, there
was a beautiful 1955 Precision Bass. This was a contoured-body bass
like Sting's, but what was truly unbelievable was the bass was a light
pink color with gold parts. Danny and I both nearly fell over. The bass
wasn't super-clean, but it was obviously original and the condition was
very good. He said it was custom-made for him. He wouldn't sell the
bass at the time, and I continued to call him from time to time, but he
would never sell it. After several years, the phone number and address
were no longer any good. It is a bass I still dream about. I won't mention
the name of the man because I don't want anyone else to find him and
buy the bass. I still have hope that if he is still around, I may one day
own this bass!

I can go on with these stories for days, but now I will tell you about
one of the biggest ones that got away. One day a friend of mine, Gerry
McGee of the Ventures, came into the store and told me that his friend
Delaney Bramlett was considering selling his all-rosewood Telecaster.
This was not just any rosewood Telecaster. This was George Harrison's
"Let It Be" rosewood Telecaster. George had "given" it to Delaney many
years before. At the time I believe Delaney needed the money. Gerry

took me to Delaney's ranch house in the valley and Delaney showed me the guitar. He had used the guitar over the years and even routed it for a humbucking pickup in the neck position.

I believe I possibly could have purchased the guitar for about $60,000. I had been aware of it for a number of years. There was a bit of lore that came with this guitar. Delaney received the guitar as a gift from George. However, I had been told that George thought of it as only a loan. I probably could have closed a deal on that particular day. My only fear was that after I purchased the guitar, George might come to me and want it back! (This was not unlikely, believe it or not. George always drove a hard bargain.) Gerry and I spent a few hours with Delaney, but I got cold feet. How could I refuse George if he wanted the guitar back? A few years later, the guitar was sold at auction for quite a bit more than $60,000. I believe it was purchased posthumously for George's wife, Olivia, by Ed Begley Jr. To this day it is back with George's other guitars in Olivia's possession, and that is a good thing.

19

MYSTERIOUS ONE-OFFS

I have been blessed to have seen, owned, and brokered some of the most exquisite examples of American guitar art in the world. I am always on the lookout to see instruments that are unique and have abnormalities of design. I've already mentioned a couple—the Eddie Cletro rosewood-necked Strat and the Freddie Tavares desert-sand Jazzmaster. These instruments have features not usually associated with the models they represent, and thus were obviously custom ordered or perhaps experimental.

I was also lucky to have gotten those Fenders from the original owners and to have learned the reasons why they ordered them. The truth is, now most of those old guys are gone, and we may never hear the firsthand story about the origins of a specific guitar or know the reasoning behind decisions that were made about it.

Another issue is that many of those guitar manufacturers changed corporate ownership over the years, and records were lost or never kept properly. Only the venerable C. F. Martin & Company, reflecting its Teutonic roots, has kept detailed records of every guitar it's ever made, utilizing sequential serial numbers to this very day!

———

Arguably, the most mysterious company is Gibson, which changed corporate ownership numerous times in the last eighty years. In fact, it's hard even to date many a Gibson. You have to check the factory order numbers, which are often impossible to see. In some ways, you have to be an archeologist to track everything the company was doing, but there's always some crazy Gibson that shows up, defying all the rules!

While Martin dominated the flat-top market, Gibson, headed by the legendary Lloyd Loar, put its energy into archtops, the iconic guitars of jazz in the big band era. Loar is the gentleman who first put violin f-holes on guitars, a design element that has remained the industry standard for jazz guitarists.

Although I love all guitars, archtops could be the instruments closest to my heart. Maybe it's because one of my first major scores was that L-5 that got crushed back in Florida when I was a young man. The care and time that goes into making them is considerable. Their construction is so much more complex than their solidbody and flat-top counterparts. Their tops are carved and individually voiced by hand. The backs and sides require subtle bending of the woods. I'm drawn to the lovely way the fingerboards are constructed and applied to the guitar's body, some flush, some raised and extended. Their bracing is complex and that, along with matching the proper woods to the instruments, creates the guitar's individual voice. No two are exactly alike. Gibson must have had its own archtop "custom shop" at work over the years, although it's hard to pinpoint when or why.

———————

Archtop lovers are often jazz players who are passionate about the tradition and enthralled with the wide variety of tones these guitars can provide, from mellow to the heavy acoustic "chop." My old friend Jim Fox is one of these guys. Jim is one of the finest all-around guitar players I

A COLLECTION

OF

NORMAN'S RARE GUITARS

Gibson Les Paul Standards

Ones that I bought, sold, or didn't have the foresight to buy.

Martin 1941 D-45

Fender 1958
Jazzmaster
Freddie Tavares
Prototype
Maple Neck

National
1930 Style
4 Round
Neck

Gibson 1960 ES-335TDN
Blonde Dot Neck

Fender
1964
Jazz
Bass
Sonic
Blue

Martin 1934 D-28
First Year

Fender 1951
Nocaster

Martin 1896-1897 0-42

Gibson 1934
Jumbo
"Gibson's
First
Dreadnaught
Acoustic"

Fender 1965
Fender
Jazzmaster
Olympic
White

*Gibson 1941 SJ-200
Rosewood Horseshoe*

Martin 1945 D-18

D'Angelico
1960 Excel

Gibson 1963 SG Les Paul Transition

Gibson 1940 L-5 Premiere

Martin 1928
000-45

Gibson 1957
Les Paul
TV Special

Guild 1964 DE-500

Gibson 1955
Les Paul
All Gold
Standard

Fender 1962 Jaguar Burgundy
Mist Metallic

Gibson 1924
L-5
Lloyd Loar
Master
Model

Gibson 1962 ES-330TDC
Transitional

Fender 1960
Jazzmaster
Blonde
Slab-Board
Gold Parts

Gibson 1940
Super 400
Premiere

Gibson 1938
J-35 Banner
Natural

Fender 1965 Jaguar Dakota Red

Gibson 1962
Hummingbird

Gibson 1959
ES-355 Mono

Gibson
1957
Les Paul
Custom
Fretless
Wonder

Gibson 1961
ES-335TD
Dot Neck
Short Guard

Gibson L5 CES
Natural Solid Body

Rickenbacker 1968
365-WB

Fender
1955
Stratocaster
Ash Body
Maple Neck

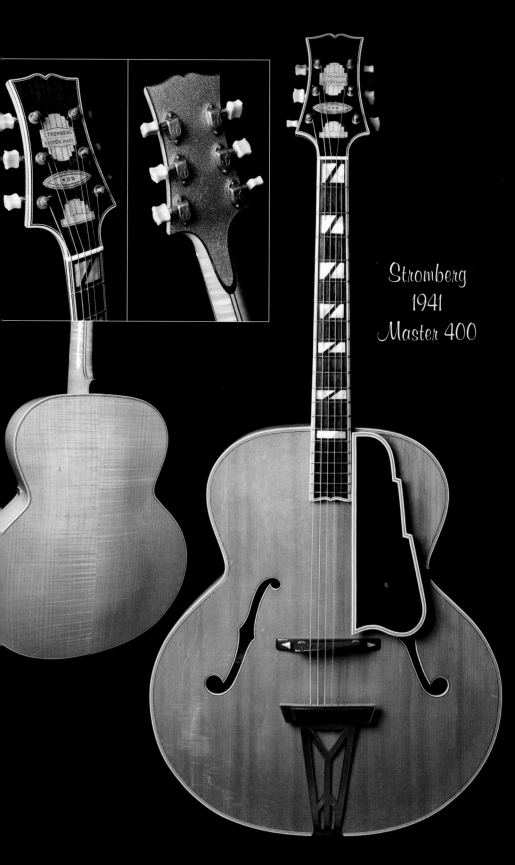

Stromberg
1941
Master 400

Gibson 1907
F4 Mandolin 3 Point

Gibson 1918
F4 Mandolin

Gibson 1916
F2 Mandolin

Presentation Mandolins

Larson Brothers
Maurer Mandolin

Larson Brothe
Stahl Mandol

Larson Brothers
Maurer Bowl
Back Mandolin

Vega Pearl Mandolin

Regal Pearl Mand

Gibson blond L-5. (Photos by Jen Angkahan)

have ever met. He is a veteran session player who has played with many of today's top stars. He's a fluid soloist, who is capable of playing some of the most astonishing single-note solos I have ever heard. Google him, and his discography will blow your mind.

However, the art that is closest to Jim's heart is the old-school acoustic rhythm playing that was so prevalent in the thirties and forties big band era. For over twenty-some years, Jim has toured and recorded with Frank Sinatra Jr. on a regular basis.

I sold Jim two Gibsons that defy all features normally associated with their models. One is a blond Gibson 1961 acoustic L-5 non-cutaway. What makes this guitar unique is that the seventeen-inch L-5 body has been fused with the classic Super 400 fingerboard inlays and a marbleized Super 400 pickguard. In other words, the features on this guitar combine the best of both models. Yet the most unusual feature is the

Gibson L-7C Special. (Photos by Jen Angkahan)

guitar's black binding, which makes the blond finish just pop out by its beautiful contrast.

By 1961, Gibson stopped making L-5 non-cutaways. In Gibson's ledger, the guitar was shipped in 1961 to Japan. This could mean the owner might have possibly been in the military or might have been an American expatriate.

The second guitar is a gorgeous Gibson L-7C with a sunburst finish. What makes this guitar unusual is the shallow depth of the body. It is basically the depth of a Byrdland. I have seen L-5CTs with thin bodies, which are referred to as the George Goebel models. The L-5CTs are extremely rare, but in all my years I have never seen an L-7CT with the thin body. The guitar is not labeled L-7CT, so I believe this was probably a one-of-a-kind custom order.

I'll let Jim Fox tell you about it, in his own words: "Dropping by Norm's store is always fun and a regular thing for many of the players around LA. Everyone there is there because they dig guitars. Perfect! I dropped by one day around 2003 and Norm said, 'I got something you should see.' He has special places for special guitars, some very secret, but this one case was under his desk in his private office. Out came this old, brown Lifton case with the soft, pink lining, but then it got bizarre. An acoustic L-5, the one Norm just described. My mind became cloudy and confused. Being very tuned in to this type of guitar, I hit a disconnect from reality. Many of the appointments on this instrument were opposite of normal, but it was spectacular!

"I said, 'Norm, what is it? Is it all-original? When did they make it? How did this happen?' On top of all this, it sounded gorgeous and was in mint condition, with a perfect oval neck and consistent sounding in all registers.

"He told me. 'Not for sale, and if it were for sale it would be crazy.' He just wanted me to check it out, knowing I dig archtops so much.

"CUT! Approximately three years later, I get a voice message from Norm. 'Jim, I've got a real cool L-7. Very different, and I'm letting a few of the cats know about it. It's a 'player.'

"I was in the neighborhood and stopped in. My good friend and great player Jon Kurnick was there checking out this thin L-7, which states 'L-7C Spec' on the interior label. I started playing this ultra-cool guitar when Jon says, 'Hey Jim, you should buy it.'

"I loved how he was trying to spend my money and egg me on, so I quipped, 'Screw you, Jon, you buy it.'

"He says, 'It's a 'one-off' and you'll never see another like it.'

"Game on. I said, 'Jon, if you want to know about super-cool one-off archtops, ask Norman about his L-5!'

"Jon said, 'Norm, tell me about this L-5.'

"'What L-5?' said Norm.

"'The crazy blond one.'

"'Oh, that one! It's in my office under my desk. I don't think I've shown it to anyone since you saw it.'

"'That was at least three years ago,' I reminded him. Out comes the L-5, you know this part by now. Jon is stunned like a deer in the headlights. Keep in mind that there are other customers wandering around, looking at regular stuff and pretending to ignore this little board meeting. After some playing and unintelligible chatter, speaking in tongues, perspiration, giggling, et cetera, Jon says once again, 'Hey, Jim, you should buy it.'

"I answered the predictable, 'Screw you *again*, Jon.' Two weeks later, with the blessing and encouragement of my wife, I bought both guitars. I cannot remember every date or appearance made with them, but the L-5 worked on my CD *Natural Blonde*, a Big Bad Voodoo Daddy record, a Frank Sinatra Jr. record, and a Steve Lawrence record, to name a few. The L-7 can be heard on Big Bad Voodoo Daddy's recording of, 'Give Me That Wine.' It's a great blues guitar and has remarkable acoustic power, especially for a thin-line. It's often with me for sessions because this guitar will do anything well.

"A quick L-5 side note: I agree with Norman that Gibson should appoint some guitars this way. It's stunning and incorporates some of the coolest features, visually. I have been terrified that this insanely beautiful centerfold L-5 would be scratched or damaged in the workplace. Studios and stages are often cramped and treacherous. I showed it to a friend who is very passionate about this stuff, like me, and he really took to it, so it now resides in the remarkable Ray Sherr Collection."

———

Another custom order or one of a kind is a Gibson L-4CE that recently

Gibson L-4CE. (Photo by Jen Angkahan)

crossed my path. This guitar is extremely rare in original black finish with a Charlie Christian Pickup. When I first looked at this guitar my initial reaction was, this can't be right. When I looked at the label inside the guitar, I discovered it read L-4CE. The *E* means factory electric. There are many L-4Cs but very, very few L-4CEs. The L-4C is the same body as the ES-175, but the top is solid spruce. The ES-175 is a ply-maple pressed top. The inlay pattern on the neck, the crown on the headstock, and all other features are identical. The body is sixteen inches, and the scale length is also identical to the 175.

It is known that the brilliant British jazz guitarist John McLaughlin

Gibson ES-355 Mono with Byrdland short scale. (Photo by Jen Angkahan)

used a black L-4CE on all of his sixties' session work. I have looked all over to find a photograph of him with this guitar (just in case) to no avail.

I purchased this guitar and sold it to my good friend and fellow archtop obsessive, co-writer David Yorkin. I feel this guitar is super-appropriate for this chapter. I assure you it sounds incredible with that Charlie Christian Pickup.

———————

Mysterious Gibson "one-offs" weren't only limited to archtops. At a trade show a number of years ago, I stumbled across a stunning mono ES-355 on display. The price was so high I just kept walking past it, thinking, I would love to own it but would rather not have the guy take a swing at me by making a lower offer.

Personally, I love the mono version of the 355 for its simplicity. Sure stereo instruments produce a great sound, but the sound path on mono guitars to the amp has less obstruction and is more "pure" to my ears.

After walking by the guitar for two days, I couldn't take it anymore. I figured, what the hell, and I chatted up the owner. I told him it was cool to be optimistic about putting a figure on a guitar, but this price seemed slightly delusional. However, if he really wanted to make a deal . . .

I took a quick look at the guitar and made an offer. After a bit of negotiation, we found some middle ground. Of course, I had to inspect it. First order of business was opening up the pickups to make sure they were P.A.F.s. This is a customary procedure. I need to be able to represent any instrument I sell accurately. (I have never been in a lawsuit, and I want to keep it that way!) After everything checked out, I paid the man and left with my acquisition. I packed it up with all the other gear I bought and got everything ready for shipping home.

A few days later, everything arrived in one piece, and I began inventorying the new stuff and photographing it for my website. However, when I looked closely at the guitar, I realized something was very strange. The pickup placement on the guitar was closer than the usual distance between the pickups! After picking it up and playing it, I realized that the scale length of the guitar was actually shorter than other standard Gibsons.

I pulled out my tape and measured the scale. I discovered that the guitar actually had a Byrdland scale. The regular scale of an ES-355 is 24 3/4, but this guitar had the very unusual scale length of 23 1/2. I had never seen a semisolid Gibson ever with this feature. It had to mean that the 355 was a one of a kind custom order!

It was pretty ironic because in my haste to buy it, I overlooked the most interesting thing about it. Everything else about the guitar was correct—the finish, the hardware, et cetera, but because I never even played the guitar, the scale length just got right by me! Usually I am a lot more careful about these things, but I was so stoked about getting it, I overlooked this pretty big detail. Lesson learned. I now take a little more time to examine all aspects of a potential sale. In this particular case, I got very, very lucky!

I sold this guitar to a good friend of mine, who resides in Canada. And if I'm still lucky, someday I hope to possibly re-broker this killer one-of-a-kind instrument.

20

THE GREATEST
UNKNOWN GUITARIST

M y master plan had always been to sell a few guitars to provide
myself a little financial freedom. I hoped eventually I would
have time to actually study guitar.

If you lived in LA and you were into guitar, there was only one person to study with—Ted Greene. I have known and done business with
some of the greatest guitarists in the world, and I can say without question that Ted was miles above them all.

Ted Greene with Blackguard Fender 1953 Telecaster.
(Photo by Bob Barry)

Through it all, he never raised his price per lesson. It was always $15 or $20, from the seventies all the way until his untimely death in 2005. Everybody studied with him, from Andy Summers to Lee Ritenour.

Ted's knowledge of chord voicings and inversions on guitar was encyclopedic and revolutionary. He had studied with George Van Eps, but we all felt he'd surpassed the master. Ted was the ultimate "chord melody" guitarist, but he damn near knew every song ever written and loved all kinds of music.

He had written a famous book in the seventies called *Chord Chemistry*, illustrating his hundreds of chord voicings. There was so much material in that book, nobody in the world could digest it! That, along with his cover photo with a thick beard and a modified cherry red ES-355, solidified his reputation as an eccentric genius, which was probably an understatement.

Ted later used to refer to his book as "Chord Catastrophe." He knew that he should have found a way to simplify all this information, but as it is, the book remains a mystifying document.

———

I met Ted through my vintage guitar business, back when I was selling out of my apartment. Ted would customize all these old guitars I'd sell him, but I couldn't really get down on him for that, because he was so brilliant and was always in search of some kind of mystery guitar sound. Later, he started to respect some of the guitars he bought a little more. He bought some Blackguard Teles from me, a Gibson Switchmaster, and toward the end, became very interested in finding and playing Guild guitars, because he felt they were a really good value for the money.

Ted was a legend out here, yet he only recorded one solo album in his lifetime. I knew him when he played with a group called the Blues-berry Jam, back in about 1970. He also used to teach at Ernie Ball's store on Ventura Boulevard, not far from where my store is now.

Ted was an iconoclast, and we all loved him for it. He was so methodical about everything. He had the smallest handwriting of anybody I've ever seen. He documented every musical discovery he ever made, which was considerable. He would spend most of his time sitting cross-legged on the floor, formulating his ideas, and writing them down. Thank God he did that, because his musical insights are available, though in a lifetime only Ted himself could master them.

Though he's known for his chord work, he was also a phenomenal single-note player. He was into doo-wop, which is where he and I found common ground. He loved the Moonglows, just like I did. He even liked the way I sang. Somewhere in my archives I have a tape of his accompanying me, but I always felt my vocals and others' were a chain around his leg. I'd rather just hear him play on his own.

He was a fascinating, creative musician, who never repeated himself—he was always improvising, coming up with mind-boggling arrangements on the fly. But he was so modest that he'd never even announce a gig. You'd have to find out from somebody else that he was playing somewhere around town. He also had a frustrating habit of backing up singers who were not on his level. I think he just wanted to take the focus off himself, which was near impossible once he had a guitar in his hands.

I remember one Tuesday night he was playing at the Baked Potato in North Hollywood. The first set was classic Ted, solo guitar at its finest. He played every part in the Percy Faith Muzak hit "Theme from a Summer Place." He covered all the string parts, and everything else, and knocked everyone out.

For the second set, he came out playing the old spiritual "Swing Low, Sweet Chariot." Well, there's nothing hip or even accessible on that tune. It was just bizarre. What made it more bizarre is that he proceeded to invite all these "singers" up on the bandstand, and each singer tried to "cut" each other by oversinging, and overemoting. It was just awful. Then he pointed to me, and I shook him off. No way was I going up there.

In some ways, he reminded me of Dylan, because you just did not know whether he was screwing with people or was being sincere about these things. I know he sincerely saw the good in everybody, but it was odd.

Once, I heard he was going to be playing at a restaurant called the Sea Shell, right up the street from my store. I went there, and there were about twenty people in the restaurant.

Ted was sitting at a table with his dad, and I'll never forget this, he had a baked potato on a plate in front of him. You could hear his guitar, but you couldn't see it. He was hiding his guitar under the table, playing while he was eating dinner. He'd hit a chord, let it ring, then take a bite of the potato! What a character. It was the nuttiest thing I've ever seen in my life.

Another time, Dan Duehren and I were at John Pisano's guitar night, and Ted was the last guy to go on. He almost always gigged with a Telecaster, which was unusual for a jazz guy, but he got a beautiful tone on it. Still, he was a perfectionist, always on the hunt for the right sound.

Pisano would introduce everybody, and he was standing there waiting to introduce Ted, but Ted was messing around with his Deluxe Reverb amplifier on stage. He'd hit a chord, get up, go to the amp, turn some knobs, go back, sit, hit another chord, get up, go to the amp, et cetera. I mean this thing went on for fifteen minutes! Finally Danny said to John, "You'd better just introduce him, or we'll be here 'til two in the morning!"

That was par for the course with Ted. He was an odd cat. He lived like a hermit in his apartment in Encino with stuff all around. I guess today you'd call him a hoarder. He was seriously into old cars, and he had car magazines and videotapes piled up to the ceiling. With all his interest in cars, the car that he drove was extremely modest. His apartment was organized, but it was also insane. You couldn't even get into one of the bathrooms, it was so jammed full of stuff. It was organized, but it was also insane.

His diet was strange—he'd eat popcorn, french fries, and M&Ms. He didn't really take care of himself, at all. He would sit in a yoga position all day, which couldn't have been good for his circulation. He took care of everybody except himself. He was always the last on the list. I know that he was an insomniac and that might've accounted for his incredible musical productivity.

The man had heart. For our twenty-fifth wedding anniversary party, he backed up the great singer Donny Gerard on Marlene's favorite James Ingram song, "One Hundred Ways." It was so beautiful, a memory permanently etched into my mind.

For all his influence, there's precious little recorded output. We begged him to record more, but he professed never to be ready. This man was more ready than any other guitar player on the planet! His perfectionism kept him from getting all his brilliance down on tape. He could've made a lot more money in music, but he just liked teaching and showing people things on the guitar. Ted would teach anybody, and he would always find something positive in a person's playing, no matter how crude it might be.

When I "studied" with him, I was really into Curtis Mayfield, and Ted liked my R&B rhythm playing. But I was always too busy to practice, so it never led anywhere. I didn't feel it was right for me to take up some other deserving student's time.

About a month before he died, he traded me a bunch of his old guitars for some Guilds. One was an early 1960s Gibson ES-345 that I held onto for many years. Ted had stuffed foam into the *f*-holes and that had reacted against the pickups. It dissolved the P.A.F. stickers. I kept that guitar in the store, with a picture of Ted playing it stuck onto the strings, until one of his students really wanted it. I figured that Ted would rather have the guitar played than just sitting there.

There is not a person who plays guitar in LA who has not been touched by Ted, directly or indirectly. It seems almost every week I meet someone who had an experience with him or is studying Ted's lessons on the Ted Greene website.

They say that genius is closely related to insanity. I guess Ted was living proof of that. The gift is that he didn't have to die to be discovered. All of us knew and honored his genius while he was still alive.

I am struck by the fact that his talent and art still looms large as the years go by. I was lucky that I got to be around when a genius like Ted was doing his thing. I won't see another one like him in this lifetime.

Ted Greene playing at Norman and Marlene's twenty-fifth wedding anniversary. (Photo by Marlene Harris)

21

FOGERTY'S RICK

Nowadays, most players change guitars as much as they change their underwear. They draw from an arsenal, and depending on the song, switch from guitar to guitar, often at a dizzying pace. Other than Willie Nelson's "Trigger," his battle-worn Martin Classical N-20, and Bruce Springsteen's early Fender Esquire/Telecaster, few musicians these days are associated with one specific guitar.

Back in the sixties and seventies, the guitar world was a different place. If you found a decent guitar, you held onto it. In fact, you played it into the ground, because it was not easy finding another one of comparable quality. Think of Eric Clapton's "Blackie," the torn-up veteran of a thousand nights of music, compared with Eric's bevy of custom shop Strats he uses at any gig in recent years.

———

Few guitars are as associated with an artist as much as John Fogerty's Rickenbacker 325. At the pinnacle of his career as the leader of Credence Clearwater Revival, he played almost exclusively his Rickenbacker 325, and a black Gibson Les Paul Custom.

Some of you youngsters might not really remember Credence too well, but for a time they produced some of rock and roll's catchiest,

John Fogerty with Rickenbacker 325. (Getty Images)

rootsiest, Top 40 hits. John Fogerty was the force behind those hits, which were mostly played on his Rickenbacker.

Long before the advent of MTV and digital video, Fogerty's Rick was featured on the most watched television variety show in the country— *The Ed Sullivan Show*. Back then, a band hadn't truly made it until they appeared on *Sullivan*. So, that Rickenbacker had a tremendous amount of notoriety.

I used to advertise on a regular basis in both *Guitar Player* magazine and *Guitar World* magazine, which exposed my store to a new clientele, both national and worldwide. At the time, these magazines featured a lot of vintage instruments as well as new ones. The magazines also featured stories about the top guitarists of the day. Occasionally I would get a call tipping me off about instruments that were for sale.

It turned out an upcoming issue was going to feature John Fogerty's Rickenbacker 325 as a centerfold. He had given it to his guitar tech and road manager years before, after John moved on to other instruments. I've noticed that it's not usually clear to the artists who play them that their instruments often mean a lot to fans and interested parties. Maybe

John Fogerty's Rickenbacker 325. (Photo by Gary Dick of Gary's Classic Guitars)

that says something about the artistic sensibility of "not looking back," or not sentimentalizing about an old guitar. Maybe John looked at the Rick as a tool, not recognizing its place in musical history. However, to anybody into Credence, the Rickenbacker was the guitar that had all the mojo.

A friend at *Guitar World* magazine said the owner was considering selling the guitar and asked if I might be interested. Because I had been a Credence fan and loved John's songs, as well as his economical guitar playing, my response was, "I certainly am." I called the seller and inquired about the guitar's condition and originality. It was described as being in good condition but had a few features that were not fully original. John had added a Gibson humbucking pickup to the body, removed the Rickenbacker nameplate truss rod cover, and added the word ACME to the cover. The humbucker was added to the guitar just prior to the *Sullivan* appearance and can be seen on YouTube videos of that performance.

Vintage guitar values are based on the year, model, and originality. Memorabilia, however, is its own unique market, with its value based on the guitar's specific history and provenance with the player. When it comes to memorabilia, originality is not always a major concern. If the modifications were made by the artist playing the instrument and history was made by the artist with the instrument, it can even add to the value. This makes the instrument unique and even more identifiable with the artist. Who wouldn't want to own a guitar played by one of music's great luminaries?

I negotiated the price with the seller and we settled at $8,500. This was a lot of money at the time, but I figured there would have to be other Fogerty fans that would want to have the guitar. I kept it for about seven or eight years, and it was featured in a number of articles.

I was contacted by a number of interested parties but really didn't have the heart to sell. Then one day, John Fogerty walked into the store, wanting to see his Rickenbacker! He waxed nostalgic as he handled his old friend. It had been decades, but I could see the guitar still had meaning to him. He asked how much I was asking for it. I told him but offered him the guitar for half of my asking price. I figured if John really wanted the guitar, I was more than happy to sell it back to him.

I also asked John about something that had baffled me. Why the ACME logo on the headstock? He said, "Weren't you a fan of the Road Runner cartoons?" We both laughed.

After thinking about it for a few days, John told me he would feel strange about paying the price for a guitar he had once given away as a gift. I totally understood. It was an unusual situation.

Shortly thereafter, my friend and fellow dealer Gary Dick, from Gary's Classic Guitars, contacted me and said he was willing to pay my asking price. This transaction was made over a decade ago, but I believe Gary still has it in his collection, to this day. The old saying, "One man's trash is another man's treasure," could not be more appropriate.

22

SCARY
SITUATIONS

The vintage guitar market has long been a business where cash is king. That said, I'm often asked if I've ever been in situations where I felt in jeopardy. For the most part, old guitars are safer than the illicit drug business. But sometimes it can get a bit sketchy . . .

In the early eighties, in response to my ad in the *LA Times*, I received a call from a man who had an old Stratocaster he wanted to sell. I asked the usual questions in trying to determine what the guitar was, in terms of age, originality, and color, to make sure I wasn't wasting my time. According to the serial number, the guitar was pre-L-Series and checked out to be mid- to late 1962. I asked about the decal as well as other features, such as tremolo, to narrow it down further. The man informed me that he was the original owner of the guitar and that his father had purchased it for him brand new.

When I asked about the color of the guitar, he said it was kind of a purple color. That perked my interest—it meant it was either a refinish or it was a very rare burgundy mist metallic custom color. I asked how much he wanted, and he said $2,500, which was substantial. He said friends told him that old Stratocasters had become quite valuable and he was firm about this price. In an anguished voice, he said he really did not want to sell the guitar because it was sentimental to him, but he needed the money. In cash.

Fender 1964 burgundy mist Stratocaster.
(Photo by Norman Harris)

I told him I would have to go to the bank to get cash, and I asked for his address. I immediately recognized that it was a tough part of East LA that I had been to before. Basically I'd rather not go back there with a pocket full of cash, but I had to check it out. A burgundy mist Strat doesn't come along every day.

When I pulled up, my memory hadn't failed me. It was a dicey area overrun by gangs and drug dealing, but the house itself looked okay. I knocked on the door, and the seller greeted me and invited me into his dining room. As I entered, the stench of stale booze wafted by me. It was pretty obvious he had been drinking because his speech was slurred and in fact he was, to put it mildly, shit-faced drunk. He was distraught over whatever problems he was experiencing in his life.

It wouldn't be the first time I dealt with a drunk person. As a matter of fact, it kind of goes with the territory in my business. As I approached his dining room table, I immediately tensed up. Laying on the very same table as the guitar was a huge machete, alongside a giant bottle of I. W. Harper Scotch.

Sizing up the situation, I saw now that the guy was pretty unstable. I also knew that he was aware I had cash on me and that he really didn't want to sell his guitar. I am a pretty big guy, and I can take care of myself pretty well, but it still was an unnerving situation. I evaluated different strategies to block that machete, if I needed to. But I had come this far . . .

The seller opened the older brown Fender hard case, and sure enough, there lay an original-finish burgundy mist Stratocaster! After quickly looking it over, I knew I wanted to buy the guitar, but I was still ill at ease over the seller's unpredictability. He told me he hated to sell the guitar but was in a financial bind and needed the $2,500. I wanted the guitar and I wanted to pay for it and get out pronto. In this situation, negotiating might be a bad idea. The sun was starting to go down, and I wasn't sure if knowing I had cash might bring some of the seller's friends to the house, and possibly something bad might happen.

As you can see, a lot was going through my mind. I quickly pulled out the cash and asked for a receipt. After I paid the man, he asked me to sit down and have a drink with him. The guitar was very nice, and I was happy to be the new owner, but I didn't want to press my luck. There was no way on earth I was going to be hanging out. I told him that my wife was preparing dinner and that if I was late, I would be in the doghouse. I shook the seller's hand, grabbed the guitar, and headed for the car as fast I could go without running.

———————

Another time, back in the eighties, I was heading to an early Texas guitar show in Dallas. I wasn't a known quantity by many of the dealers around the country, and the only way to make deals was to bring a lot of cash. Knowing that, I went to the bank several times, socked money away, and after a few months had accumulated a little over $30,000. Even today that's a lot of money, but back then, $30,000 bought a lot of guitars. I believe at the time you could have purchased the nicest 1950s Sunburst Les Paul Standard for under $5,000.

I packed light and took a carry-on bag with me on board the plane. I had stuffed the dough inside several pairs of athletic white socks in my carry-on bag. (This was before 9/11 when hardly anybody searched anything at airports.) I was on board the plane shooting the shit with a friend, and I had my bag stashed down by my feet.

Just before take off, the flight attendant spotted the carry-on bag by my feet and said that I would have to check the bag in with the luggage. I immediately panicked! I couldn't exactly announce to the plane that there was over $30,000 in there. I am sure many people have been killed for much less. The flight attendant assured me that the bag would be waiting for me at the baggage claim after the flight. I didn't know what to do, so after an agonizing minute, I handed it to her. Upon arrival, I went to the baggage claim and discovered that my bag was nowhere to be found.

I almost had a nervous breakdown. I had no bag and no money to buy guitars at the show. I went into the lost baggage office and explained that the flight attendant made me check in my bag. Of course, I didn't mention the money, but I said that my clothes, toiletries, and necessary items were in the bag. They probably thought I was a little wacko to be so upset over those little things, but I didn't care. The man in the lost baggage office traced my bag and was able to determine that it did not make it onto my flight and would arrive at the airport the following morning.

Needless to say, I got absolutely no sleep that night. I figured the odds were that I would never see that money again, and I would have no way of buying guitars at the show. It would take a very long time for me to make up that great of a loss.

After a sleepless night, I used the last money in my pocket to take a cab to the airport the following morning. I went to the lost baggage office and anxiously awaited the arrival of my bag. I knew what flight it was supposed to be on, and I wanted to be there as soon as it arrived. After waiting about twenty minutes, a man came walking out carrying my bag. That didn't ease my nerves. I did not want to check for the money in front of the people in the office, but I was sure it had to have been stolen.

As soon as I left the office, I broke open the bag. I checked my socks and sure enough the money was still inside. I could not believe my luck. I was so wound up thinking that I was never going to see my money again. It was like giving birth trying to get through the night waiting for my bag to arrive!

I had a good show and purchased quite a few guitars over the next few days, but this was an experience I will never forget. Now that I'm more well known, people accept my checks. It's a credit card world now, so I don't have to worry about such things happening again. Nevertheless, old-timers like me remember when cash was king, but dealing with royalty has its risks.

Contestant's name _____ Age ____ Parent's ____

Address _____ City/State _____

Phone _____ Email _____

WING LUKE
MUSEUM

The Seattle Times

FREEMAN FOUNDATION

CENTURYLINK
FIELD

ROBERT G
FOUNDATIO

23

KILLER
BASSES

The Fender Bass will forever be the sound that defined R&B, the music I love above all other genres. I have been fascinated by Fender basses ever since I bought that first early 1962 Jazz Bass from Frank Williams.

Back in 1975, at my store's first location, a man came in carrying a vintage Fender Bass case. He asked if I was buying older instruments and said he had one that he was no longer using. He opened the case and revealed an early split pickup Precision Bass with an anodized pickguard and a maple neck. The bass had a white finish, but what was most peculiar was that it also had a matching white headstock. This was common on Jazz basses, but I'd never seen this on a Precision Bass before. Everything appeared original, but this was highly unusual.

So I started asking questions. First off, I asked him how he got the bass. He said he was the original owner and that it had been made for him by Leo Fender. That got my attention. His name was Rue Barkley, and he said he played bass with one of the great early legends of electric guitar, Jimmy Bryant. I knew that Jimmy Bryant was one of the first endorsers of Leo's Telecaster and played a huge part in putting Fender on the map.

We discussed price and eventually came up with something mutually agreeable. I bought the bass and kept it for almost forty years. It was

Fender 1958 Precision Bass with
matching headstock. (Photo by
Jen Angkahan)

featured in my first book and has appeared in numerous publications.
It was a beautiful one-off. It was lightweight. It played and sounded
great and had wonderful provenance, even though I had no photos to
prove it. Now with the Internet, and YouTube, I was able to come up
with pictures and even an early video of Rue playing the bass with the
great Jimmy Bryant. If you haven't heard of Jimmy Bryant, you really
need to check him out. He was far ahead of his time. He had blazing
speed and articulation, and had amazing taste in his playing. He was
known as "the fastest guitarist in the West," and quite possibly could be

responsible for the Telecaster being the ubiquitous lead guitar sound in country music!

I was never interested in selling the bass. But it got so much attention and notoriety, I knew eventually I'd have to part with it. Recently, Geddy Lee, bassist and keyboardist with Rush, wanted to know what was going on with it. I told Geddy I still had the bass and he said he was very interested. Geddy lives in Canada and we communicated through the Internet. We came up with a price that worked for both of us, and he is now the owner of one of the coolest precision basses I've ever played. What was also interesting is in the early videos of Bryant, everyone in the band was using matching white instruments and you can clearly see the P-Bass in action. I'm sure Geddy will get great use out of the bass and make his own history with it, from one legend to the next.

═════════

A while back, when I used to cold-call musicians through the Local 47 handbook, I made contact with a woman named Alice Ripatti. She lived in Woodland Hills with her sister Barbara. I asked her my usual questions, and she said she had a few instruments that she was willing to part with.

When I arrived, she informed me that in the fifties she had a band with her sisters and they used to play Las Vegas. I believe there may have been a third sister in the band. They hadn't played music in many years but like many musicians, they continued to pay their union dues to keep them in good standing with the musicians union. They told me that their band's manager had purchased the group's beautiful, professional equipment. They were fully equipped, but the band shortly thereafter stopped playing and never picked up their instruments again.

They proceeded to pull out some unbelievable guitars, including a 1955 Gibson Les Paul Custom black with one alnico pickup and one

P-90 pickup. The guitar still had its original hangtags and was like new. Alice, who was the bass player, pulled out a 1955 Fender Precision Bass. This was just like the bass Sting is known for playing, but it was also like brand new. It had hangtags and was in its original brown gig bag.

I had never seen anything so clean. The neck had not turned yellow and was the whitest looking maple neck I had ever seen. Alice said the neck was too big for her so she barely played it. They also had a couple of minty tweed Fender amps including a 1950s Fender Bassman amp with one 15-inch speaker. I negotiated the best deal I could. The prices were not cheap. They knew what they had, those Ripatti girls, but I was determined not to leave without those instruments. I still have the bass to this day, and it is truly unbelievable. It has to be the mintiest 1955 P-Bass in existence!

Fender 1955 P-Bass. (Photos by Jen Angkahan)

24

PLAYING
FOR LAUGHS

P art of the fun of my job has been hanging out with musicians most of my life. I think there's something in the fact that they "play" guitar—there's a childlike sense of play at work in most guitar players that can lighten up the darkest situation. That goes for many people associated with the music world, including repairmen.

One of the memorable characters I met when I first came to Los Angeles was Milt Owens, the repairman to the stars. His was the only game in town. By the time I got to LA, Milt was working out of M. K. Stein Music in Hollywood, directly across from the Musician's Union, which is still there. He previously worked at legendary guitarist Barney Kessel's store, as well as Wallich's Music City. Milt was the luthier who modified Barney's Gibson ES-350, by putting on a Charlie Christian Pickup. With the many endorsements that Barney had with Kay and Gibson, you only ever saw him playing with that beat-up old ES-350!

Everyone who was anyone used Milt for guitar repair. I'm convinced part of his appeal was his ebullient personality. He was a super-likable guy who loved to talk to everyone. As a matter of fact, I hardly ever saw him do a lick of work, but he certainly knew how to make guitars play well. By today's standards, I don't know how well he would rate, because for vintage instruments, you always want to keep them as original as possible. Milt was only concerned with the guitar's playability, not its originality. They were tools to be used.

Milt also had a huge love for Kirin beer. Depending on how much he drank, his work could range from super-clean, to marginal. Milt and I got along very well, and Milt referred lots of people to me when I was getting started.

Milt would always have beautiful guitars on display, which would really catch my attention. One was a small body Gibson 1920s L-5, which had the name *Groucho* inlaid on the fingerboard. I still don't know if this was the same guitar featured in the famous canoe scene in the Marx Brothers movie, *Horse Feathers*. It could have been, or it may possibly have been another guitar owned by Groucho, (yes, Groucho did play). A friend of mine named Vblotto Zackaar purchased the guitar from Milt. Vblotto at one time played with Frank Zappa, and the Mothers of Invention. I have tried to buy this guitar from Vblotto countless times over the years, but he refused to sell it. Vblotto, who owns a shopping center near my original store, definitely does not need the money!

Milt also prominently displayed a photograph of a topless girl band playing clear Dan Armstrong plexi guitars, with everything showing. He was so irreverent. Even in the women's lib era of the seventies, women remained charmed by him. Toward the end of Milt's life, when he was probably about seventy-five, he married a much younger woman. My guess is he went out with a smile.

=====

Another one of the incredible characters I've spent time with was the great session guitarist Tommy Tedesco. You probably already know he was the most recorded guitar player of all time, as a part of the famous Wrecking Crew. Tommy was a fantastic musician, the best sight reader ever. He was also a habitual gambler, but you couldn't help loving him.

One day, he showed up and said, "Hey, Norm, I'm going to a session and all my guitars are tied up in cartage. I need a cheap classical guitar for a session. What do you have?"

I said, "Tommy, I just got this inexpensive classical in that plays and sounds really good. It might be just what you need." I pulled it out.

Tommy picked up the guitar, played a few licks on it, and said, "This'll do. How much?"

"A hundred bucks."

He said, "Norm, I know you play gin. I'll play you a game to two hundred and I'll pay you zero or two hundred bucks if I lose."

I knew I probably didn't have a chance, but what the hell? It was Tommy, after all. You can't help but like the guy. I figured if I lost it would be a good story. We played the game to 200 points, and it must have been my lucky day. I beat him badly. He immediately pulled out the $200, paid his debt, and took off to the session with the guitar.

———

Anyone who remembers our early store knows that it was not your typical guitar store. We took our guitars very seriously, but we also liked the place to feel very relaxed and free. For instance, we had a ping-pong table in the middle of the store and used to have storewide tournaments. It stayed there until a guitar got damaged while I was trying to make a diving return on a shot, and I saw the error of my ways.

Next we set up a pinball machine. We gambled $25 per game. It soon went up to $50 per game. I was doing so badly and losing so much money, I picked up the vacuum cleaner and broke the machine. I figured it was cheaper to destroy the machine than to keep it around.

We gambled on everything from bicycle races around the block to shooting baskets on the mini-basketball machine in the bar down the street. At any time you could have walked in and found a full-on poker game in progress with cards and money on the floor. I suppose we could have been shut down and arrested at any given time.

I remember one poker game when Dan Duehren had a full house. He thought he had it won, until I revealed I had 4 threes. Both were very unusually high hands, but I was the winner. Dan lost his shit, ripped up the deck, and went down the street to the liquor store to buy a new deck.

While Dan was out there, I sent young Rob, who worked at the store, to the 7-Eleven across the street to buy a big gulp. We filled the cup with ice water and placed it on top of the slightly ajar front door. When Dan came in, he pushed the door open, showing the new deck. The ice water came down on him, a direct hit! He stood there drenched, holding his new deck of cards. After we played some more poker, I took the cards out and carefully placed 4 threes under Dan's windshield wiper facing the driver, as an end of the day reminder of my big hand!

Yes, we were always so mature. We loved playing tricks on young Rob. We'd tell him that we threw something up on the roof. After he climbed up, we would remove the ladder and leave him stuck on the roof for an hour or so. Rob loved to look at girls across the street with a pair of binoculars. One day my son, Jordan, took a magic marker and traced around the viewer so that when Rob put the binoculars down, he had two black eyes. He walked around all day unaware that he looked like a raccoon.

We did everything from whoopee cushions to fart machines that we taped under stools so when musicians came in to try guitars, we pushed the button, and then we all looked at the player as if to say we heard that. One memorable day, Aerosmith came in and we activated our fart machine. Of course, Steve and Joe got a kick out of it and wanted to take it for themselves. But I wouldn't let them have it.

I also had purchased a dog leash from Disneyland that had nothing at the end of the leash, like an invisible pet. It had a control with four buttons on it. One made a dog barking sound, another a cat meowing, another a chicken noise, and the other a cow mooing. We rigged the leash so that the controller was behind the desk and the noises came from our back wall.

One day, my buddy Dave Amato from REO Speedwagon came by, and we pressed the cat's meowing noise. It sounded like it was coming from behind the wall. Dave said, "Can you hear that cat?"

I said, "Yeah, there is a cat that got stuck in the wall. Don't worry, Dave. It's been there for about two weeks. He's bound to die soon."

Dave was disgusted by my inhumanity "Hell, let's get him out of there."

"Don't worry, it will be over soon!"

Dave started freaking out, and we continued pushing the button to make the cat meow noise. We did this for a while and Dave was about to lose it, when we pushed the cow noise button, then the chicken noise button. Dave was ready to kill us, but it was all in a day's fun.

We used to love to play tricks on my English friend Chris. Like so many Brits, he was obsessed with American culture, in all forms. He had a beautiful 1962 Ford Thunderbird, which he was in love with.

One day, when he was visiting, we opened a can of sardines and left it under the driver's seat. We all watched when he got into his car to leave. Needless the say, he shot out of there like he'd been zapped with a cattle prod! Then he went crazy trying to find the source of the stench. When he finally discovered the sardines, we were literally on the floor, laughing so hard we were practically convulsing.

I guess the point is, even though we take our guitars seriously, it's important not to take ourselves too seriously. One of the reasons I got into this business is not to feel as though coming to work is a chore. If there's room for good-natured laughs, all the better. I've been the butt of quite a few pranks myself, but can't seem to remember them at this moment!

25

A REALLY
GOOD GUY

W hen I first started collecting and selling guitars, originality was not the prime consideration for most guitar traders. The market was focused on instruments that played and sounded good, regardless of their originality, as well as affordable guitars that did their job.

In order to distinguish myself, I figured that finding prime examples of certain instruments would probably be my best move. Sure, I wanted instruments that played and sounded great, but I also wanted guitars that were the least tampered with. I was using my own limited finances at the time, and I didn't want a buyer to have anything negative to say about my product. I wasn't interested in having just historically interesting instruments that didn't play.

My instincts turned out to be right, as these original examples were destined to become my most valuable instruments. Sometimes it's hard to let go of them, but if one of my friends is really in need of something outstanding . . .

———

One day a while back I received a phone call at the store from my friend, the great guitarist Richie Sambora. Richie wanted to buy Jon Bon Jovi a killer gift for his birthday and figured a vintage guitar would fit the bill.

He wasn't sure if he wanted something that was acoustic or electric, and he knew I had a lot of stuff.

Throughout his career, Jon played mostly utility non-vintage instruments. Richie wanted this to be a special gift that would introduce Jon to the virtues and beauty of vintage guitars. I love hearing this and am always happy to oblige.

We went through loads of options, both electric and acoustic, and Richie ultimately decided that an acoustic would be best. We dug deep into my collection, and he test-drove loads of vintage Martins, both Dreadnoughts, as well as some smaller 00 and 000 models, in rosewood and mahogany. Some Gibsons were also in the running, but Richie felt that a large body Martin would be the best choice to shine the "vintage light," so to speak.

Eventually he settled on a Martin D-18, feeling that the dry, yet bright and even tone of mahogany would lend itself to recording better. He of course wanted something clean and original, but he also wanted a big and balanced sound. We all know that the D-18 fills the bill in almost all aspects, and there's a reason why it is the sound we've all heard on thousands of recordings!

At the time, I had a number of D-18s in stock. I had examples from the forties, fifties, and sixties to choose from. We went through dozens of guitars, but Richie settled on an early-1950s D-18. The guitar had everything. It was super-clean and was one of the best sounding 1950s D-18s I had ever come across.

Richie also knew that Jon was a big fan of Bob Dylan. He had known Bob for some time and thought if he could get Bob to sign the guitar for Jon that this would make it an extra special gift. Richie bought the guitar, then promptly made an appointment to see Bob and bring him the guitar to sign.

About two weeks went by, and I wondered how Jon had liked the guitar. The phone rang. It was Richie, and before I could ask how it went, he was cracking up, telling me he needed a second Martin D-18 that was equal to the quality of the first!

Can you guess what happened? When Richie got together with Bob and asked him to sign the guitar, Bob started playing it and said, "Richie, I've got to have this guitar." Bob knew it sounded fantastic and asked Richie if he could buy this D-18 and if it was possible for him to choose another guitar for him to give to Jon!

Richie, like all of us, felt, "how can you say no to Bob Dylan?" So, Richie sold it to Bob at his cost and went back to the drawing board in finding another Martin D-18 for Jon. He was running out of time, as Jon's birthday was rapidly approaching. I told him to give me a day to come up with something.

Almost simultaneously, I received a call from a collector who had a number of instruments to sell. He was cashing out for the usual reasons, probably to remodel his house. Among the instruments this person had to sell was another near mint, amazing sounding early 1950s D-18. He had purchased the guitar from me about ten years previous, and I remembered it well.

Somehow in my life luck has played a huge part in my success. Whenever I sell a fine guitar, I always look to replace it with something comparable or better. Otherwise, I would probably spend the money on something, and my stock would be depleted. I always wanted to reinvest my money in other fine instruments

I immediately called Richie and told him about the guitar, and Richie flew over to my store. After playing it for a couple minutes, Richie immediately fell in love with it, bought it, and happily went on his way back to hook up with Dylan. He was a little hesitant, but he figured Bob wouldn't want both D-18s! He was right.

Mission accomplished. Bob signed the guitar, and Richie gave it to

Kyle and June Grady with the guys from Norman's Rare Guitars. (Photo by Jen Angkahan)

Jon, who flipped over it. As fate would have it, both Bob and Jon ended up with great guitars handpicked by Richie, and Richie was able to give Jon a gift that was a lifelong "keeper."

———

Dealing with fine instruments and living in Los Angeles has exposed me to some of the biggest names in the music business. I have seen many groups as they climb up the ladder, as well as quite a few going in the other direction. Some of these folks have great talent, and some have some strong peculiarities. Some make you feel a little bit in awe of them, and others do their best to make everyone feel comfortable around them, even though the general public may be a little star struck.

One day a young man named Kyle Grady came into the store with his mom, June. I could see that he had undergone some serious surgery on his face. His mom explained that Kyle had a very rare type of cancer and they thought they had it under control. Kyle seemed like such a nice kid, and I could see how much his mother loved and supported him in everything he did. Having my own children, I could not even imagine the pain she must have gone through.

Kyle mentioned that he knew I was friends with Richie Sambora. He handed me a CD of his own guitar playing and asked if I would possibly give it to Richie. He told me that while he was going through his grueling treatments, the only thing that had gotten him through his ordeal was listening to Richie's guitar playing.

I told him I'd be happy to give the CD to Richie, but could make no promises of what Richie's response might be. Then I got an idea. I told Kyle and his mom to hang out for a second while I went into my office to make a phone call. I called Richie and ran down the situation to him. I explained what the kid had been through and asked him if he might say a couple of words of encouragement to Kyle over the phone. Richie said, "Are they still there, at the store?" I told him they were. "Keep them there," he said. "I will be right over."

I don't know how many rock stars would do this, and you can't help but love a guy with such a big heart. Richie came by and, needless to say, Kyle was ecstatic. The two ended up keeping in touch, and I know they texted each other often.

When someone has such an opportunity to bring happiness into another person's life like Richie did, it shows the true character of a man. It made a big difference in Kyle's life, and he was so happy to show his buddies texts he'd gotten from his new pal Richie.

Later that year, Richie was honored by The Midnight Mission for the work he had done helping the homeless. The event took place at the Beverly Hilton Hotel. I sent Kyle and his mom plane tickets to come out and be at the event honoring Richie. Kyle was able to spend some time with Richie and me, and I know this was one of the highlights of Kyle's life.

Not long after, I was informed that Kyle went in for a checkup and found out that his cancer had reappeared. It had spread and a short time later, Kyle passed away. We were all devastated. Kyle was such an inspirational young man. He never complained about his situation.

Kyle was one of the most unforgettable characters I have ever met, and his courage will always be inspirational to me. His time on earth was cut way too short. As for Richie, I feel everyone should know what kind of man he really is. Of all the celebrities and rock stars I have ever dealt with, he is the one with the biggest heart.

Kyle Grady with Richie Sambora at the Golden Heart Awards for The Midnight Mission. (Photo by Marlene Harris)

26

REO
DAVE

The nature of the vintage guitar business is that it appeals to a select few. Its club members are enthusiastic, but most people, including many guitarists, aren't familiar with the vintage mindset. I believe that once a player gets his or her hands on a quality vintage instrument, they will be bitten by the bug like all of us!

The vintage guitar market is a direct result of the dismal state of the American guitar industry since the seventies. It seemed like the manufacturers had lost touch with the needs and wants of professional players. The major companies had figured out how to make great guitars even through the late sixties, but they all focused too much on the bottom line, and how they could save on materials and workmanship to cut costs. There were shortages in quality tone woods and other guitar-making materials.

During the seventies, foreign manufacturers figured they could do as good or better in making guitars than American companies, and they went out to prove it. Ibanez and Yamaha made some pretty good guitars, and soon enough began taking away business from the American major companies. Gibson, Fender, and Martin, to some extent, scrambled, trying to come up with "new" designs. Does anybody remember the Gibson Marauder or the Fender Bronco?

Companies like Ibanez "got it," though. They produced models that were based on the classic original Gibson designs. These later became known as "lawsuit" models. From Les Pauls to Flying Vs, from ES-175s to Johnny Smiths and L-5s, the Japanese made pretty good copies. They were also far less expensive than the American made Gibsons. Takamine's copies of Martins were likewise pretty good guitars that flooded the US market. Aria made models based on Fenders and also began to take business away from the American big three.

In the early eighties, prices on vintage American models escalated, and the big American companies began realizing that one of their biggest competitors was themselves! As a result, they began to make reissues of their own original designs. The early reissues were pretty good, and the companies realized they needed to reestablish themselves as the standard of excellence in design and quality. As the years went on, the American majors took back the big market share of the guitar-buying public.

———

Through our connections to the majors, Norman's Rare Guitars tried to advise the major companies how to help improve the quality of their products to make guitars authentic to their original designs. I often would let them inspect the vintage instruments in my collection so that they could build the best reissue possible. Gibson, Fender, Martin, and Rickenbacker did guitars to our specs, and we tried to point out the little things that the companies were overlooking or didn't think were important.

Players would show up at the store, wanting to check out these new reissue guitars and stack them up against the old. One of the first of these players was Dave Amato. Dave is an excellent guitar player and singer, and is a true believer in the vibe and mojo of vintage instruments. He was an early convert who wants other people to "see the

Gibson 1967 Byrdland with factory master
volume. (Photo by Jen Angkahan)

vintage light." He also purchased many of our reissue guitars that we
were involved in helping to redesign.

When I first met him, he was playing and singing with Ted Nugent.
Over the years, Dave would come in regularly and has built an impres-
sive collection. But they don't just hang on the wall. He plays and records with them, avidly.

Dave hooked us up with Ted Nugent and, of course, Ted bought several early Byrdlands from us. The short-scaled, hollow-bodied, carved-
topped Gibson Byrdland was an unusual choice, but he definitely made
it work for him. In fact, it gave Ted quite an unusual look back in the

seventies, when it seemed everybody else was playing Les Pauls. It was a brilliant branding strategy that has paid off, as Gibson has reissued their own "Ted Nugent Byrdland."

———

For the last twenty-plus years, Dave has played guitar with REO Speed-wagon, replacing Gary Richrath, who was another early customer. Before that, he played with Cher for quite a while, and being from the Boston area, he was friendly with a lot of big bands that probably had no idea what Norman's Rare Guitars was. But they would soon find out. Dave showed up one day with Brad, Joe, and Steven from Aerosmith. I believe they were impressed with our selection, and I think they liked the loose vibe that we had.

Dave Amato also first brought Richie Sambora to the store. In fact, I think it was Dave who convinced Richie that he needed some vintage guitars. He said, "Just check it out, I think you'll dig them." And dig them he has.

One day Richie was in the store and was looking at a pretty expensive guitar. At the same time, Dave was looking at a 1954 Stratocaster. I pulled Dave aside and told him that if Richie purchased the guitar, I would sell him the 1954 for $7,500. At the time, 1954 Stratocasters were going for about $10,000. Of course Dave went to work on Richie, and they both left with great guitars. Both of the guitars they walked away with have appreciated greatly, so they're not hurting.

Through the years, Dave also turned us on to Keith Nelson from the band Buck Cherry, Derek St. Holmes from the Ted Nugent Band, Tommy Shaw and the boys from Styx, and so many others I can't count them all. Recently Brad Whitford came to LA to play a show. Brad and Dave were hanging out in town and had a few hours to kill. What else would Dave say but "Let's go to Norm's."

Dave, Kevin Cronin, and the REO guys were even kind enough to play a gig for The Midnight Mission (LA's premier homeless shelter). Dave is good people and has a lot of friends that are good folks as well. Thanks again, Dave Amato, our number-one advocate!

27

A PIECE OF
THE MAGIC

I t's no surprise that as music fans age, the market for memorabilia
has only increased. A lot of this is due to nostalgia, as people want
to own something that is directly connected to the art or music that affected them so deeply as kids.

Another reason is that rock and roll has created its own culture and
style, which has impacted all sorts of people around the globe. Now I've
been around long enough to see all the different stages of rock style—
from psychedelia, to punk, to metal, to grunge, and all of their hybrids
and rediscoveries. Kids find their identities in these subcultures. As kids
become adults, that earlier, more innocent time in their lives becomes a
precious commodity.

Nowhere has the rock and roll culture been marketed so well as in
the Hard Rock Café. In 1979, the Hard Rock started using guitars and
other equipment like wallpaper in their restaurants. But these weren't
just "any" guitars—they had to be associated with an artist, and there
would be a full display, with guitars, photographs, clothing, and the like.
However, fully authenticating these pieces was another thing.

The original curator for the Hard Rock memorabilia was Warwick
Stone, who worked closely with co-founder Peter Morton. Eventually,
he started coming to me, looking for guitars that had been used by my
celebrity customers.

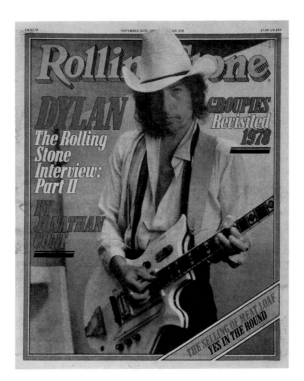

Rolling Stone's cover of Bob Dylan with National 1964 Glenwood. (Copyright © Rolling Stone LLC 1978. All Rights Reserved. Used by Permission.)

Earlier, I had traded for a 1964 National Glenwood map-shaped guitar from Bob Dylan and had him sign it. The Hard Rock was looking for something related to Bob, and I told them about the National. They were very excited, and we made a deal on it for $2,500.

I just happened to have the guitar in my window at the old store when Don Vargas, a well-known Hollywood costume designer, stopped in, saw the guitar, and informed me that he had sold it to Dylan. Then he said, "Did you know that's the guitar Dylan's holding on the cover of the *Rolling Stone* back in 1978?"

I couldn't believe it. Sure enough, Don returned the next day with the magazine, and there was Bob, wearing a cowboy hat and holding the white National!

The most important detail about any memorabilia is provenance, which is proof that the artist actually owned the piece. Now that there was the *Rolling Stone* as evidence, I could've sold the National for five times the price.

I called up the Hard Rock and told them about the cover. I said the value of the guitar had increased greatly but that I would hold to our original deal. The Hard Rock executives were so struck by this, next thing I knew they flew me to New York, put me up in a fine hotel, and had me meet everybody in person. I guess they were happy to find somebody they could trust, in a world that operates somewhat sketchily at times.

Later, they put out a book of their memorabilia, which had a bunch of questionable stuff in it. Someone had sold them a fake Tom Petty jacket, and Tom's manager, Tony Dimitriades, contacted them and told them to pull it.

By then, Don Bernstein was their curator, and knowing I had done business with Tom, asked if I could facilitate some sort of trade with Tom. I was able to rustle up some stage guitars of his—a Vox Phantom, a Rickenbacker, and some Guild acoustics, as well as some legitimate stage clothing. These were authentic items he had used on stage and could be documented. Everybody was happy.

———

As the Hard Rock Empire grew, I figured out ways to get my hands on memorabilia they could use. A rock star would come into the store to check things out, and I'd have one of my coworkers stall him or her while I made a call to the Hard Rock to see if they had an interest in "so-and-so." If I got the green light, I'd negotiate for some clothing or an instrument on the spot, then sell it to the Hard Rock. You have to strike when the iron is hot.

It was fascinating to see the things they wanted and the things they weren't interested in at all. I had contact over the years with many of the seminal people in the rock 'n' roll and blues area, but some great artists (who will remain nameless) were too esoteric for the Hard Rock buyers!

One of the funniest episodes occurred when a teen idol from the seventies showed up in the store one day. I was not sure about making the call, but I did it anyway. By then, the curator was a younger woman.

"I know this might be unusual, but do you have any interest in David Cassidy?"

Well, she went right through the roof! It shows that I was a little out of sync with the audience that grew up watching *The Partridge Family*.

That just goes to show, you never know what is going to be valuable or desirable over the years. One man's trash, indeed, is another man's treasure. Sometimes literally. Brian Ranks, former road manager to David Lee Roth and Michael Bolton, came to me one day asking if I was interested in any of David Lee Roth's stage costumes. Knowing the mania for all things Van Halen, I told him I was very interested.

"Good, because David told me to get rid of all this shit, one way or another. There are piles and piles of it."

Brian was at David's estate in Pasadena, and as he pulled up, all the gardeners and day laborers working there were wearing Roth's costumes! David just couldn't wait to unload all that stuff. Luckily, a few things were left for me.

———

In the end, all of us involved in music in whatever capacity are just fans, anyway. We love the artists, and we love their art. Everybody's got a focus on a specific thing. For me, I would be into collecting Little Beaver memorabilia, but good luck finding any! I'm sure I'm the only person in the world who would collect somebody so obscure, but he has deep meaning for me.

Occasionally, I've been able to use a musician's obsession with another artist to get something I wanted out of a situation. A number of years ago, I bought a Rickenbacker 360 double-bound Rose Morris twelve-string from my British friend Chris, which had previously been purchased at Hessy's Music Store in Liverpool. Everyone in the know knows that type of guitar is associated with the Beatles in their mid-sixties phase. What made this guitar exceptional is that it also came with its original sales receipt from Hessy's in Liverpool from 1966, which is where the Beatles bought all of their early instruments!

Well, I showed this guitar to Tom Petty, and he was practically salivating. As they are for many of us, the Beatles are his holy grail. Every time I'd see Tom, he asked how much I wanted for it, but I'd never sell it to him. This went on for years.

Finally, I told him I was willing to let go of it. He was champing at the bit, but a little hesitant over the price I was about to charge him. The deal was, I offered to trade him the guitar in exchange for several of his stage-played guitars and stage-worn clothing. I said there was one more condition. I wanted him to play a benefit concert that I was organizing at the Malibu Performing Arts Center for The Midnight Mission (homeless shelter). He was happy to oblige. Not only that, he reunited his first group, Mudcrutch, (in which he played bass) for the show! We raised over a quarter million dollars that night.

By the way, the last time I saw that Rick, Tom was performing with it at the halftime show for the Super Bowl.

I guess some memorabilia does actually get played . . . by the right person, too.

28

UNEXPECTED GIFTS

In order to keep up a supply of good guitars to satisfy my customers, I have had to develop scouts who are willing to travel around the country in search of quality guitars. It has to be someone who is trustworthy, as well as knowledgeable enough to be aware of what he or she is looking at.

I have had several people do this for me over the last couple of decades. Generally these folks should have money to invest on their own and must be willing to keep the guitars in question if they make a mistake. They sniff out the thrift shops, yard sales, any and every place an old guitar might show up, all over the country. A few times I've received calls from these scouts, telling me they've hit the "mother lode." If there were enough guitars in play, I would either fly out to inspect the instruments personally or sometimes wire money to my scout to finance the purchase. A couple of times, I sent six-figure amounts to these scouts to close the deals.

One of my guys had purchased hundreds of guitars for me without any problems. This particular friend just happened to be more familiar with electric guitars than acoustic. Out on the road a while back, he was offered a couple of high-end Martin guitars. One was a 1942 model 000-28 Herringbone. The other was a 1940 D-28 Herringbone. He knew I'd want them, so he purchased the guitars with me in mind.

When he brought the guitars to my store, I first looked at the 000-28 and was quite pleased. It was a very nice, straight guitar. When I refer to a guitar as "straight," I mean it is authentic and original, without any modifications.

However, when he presented the D-28 to me, I immediately sensed something was wrong. Sometimes, you have go with "feel," and my gut told me that something was fishy about this guitar. I checked it out, and the first thing that struck me was that the spacing in the serial numbers did not look correct. After further examination, I discovered the guitar to be a forgery, though a pretty good one, at that.

Unfortunately, this goes with the territory in the world of collectibles. When values go high enough, there will inevitably be unscrupulous people who'll go out of their way to make copies that only an expert could detect. This particular Martin was, in fact, not a Martin at all! I had to reject it, making my scout "eat" the $8,000 he dropped on the fraudulent Dreadnought. I felt bad about that, but "business is business." In the end, I bought the 000-28 and both of us made some money on the guitar, but he was in the red with that fake D-28.

We didn't do a whole lot of business after that, but he would still bring me stuff that I might be interested in from time to time. An inveterate thrifter, he was not always discriminating enough about the music-related items he bought.

He came across a pawnshop that was going out of business and ended up buying its whole musical inventory! He showed up at my store, schlepping over this big, old Thomas organ from the sixties he'd found there. The thing weighed a ton, and it didn't even work. I wouldn't even let him take it off the truck. I sell guitars, so even if I wanted it, it really didn't fit in with the store. He parked it somewhere in the back of his own store.

About six months after that, he had some time on his hands and figured he'd take a crack at fixing that damn organ. It couldn't have been too complicated, maybe a couple of blown tubes, or the like. He pulled out his tube tester and screwdriver and opened up the back of the organ to check it out.

Inside was a pouch that a previous owner had stashed back there. He opened the pouch and, lo and behold, it was filled with gold coins! Whoever had owned the organ had used it as a place to hide gold, knowing nobody would look inside. Talk about buried treasure! I was a little jealous that I hadn't been the one to get it, but I sure was happy he landed that gold. Gold was about $400 an ounce at that time. He sold it all wholesale and made about $20,000.

Talk about good karma. The universe watches over all of us, in unseen ways. The tabloids are in the business of digging up as much negative stuff as they can about celebrities and people in the public eye. I understand. Bad news sells. However, living in Los Angeles, and dealing with many celebrities, has mostly been a pleasure for me. Some of these folks are fine people—in fact, true "menschs" from my experience. Let me give you an example.

———

An incident happened a few years ago that has taken an unexpected twist. A good friend of mine, Steve Zimmerman, called me and asked me to take care of his friend, who would be coming in. That good friend just happened to be movie star Harrison Ford. He told me that Harrison was going to drop by because he wanted to buy a guitar for a good friend. I assured Steve I would look after Harrison and give him a good deal.

Later that afternoon, Harrison dropped in with another man. I had actually met Harrison years before, but he might not have remembered me. He was so low-key that not too many people recognized him off the bat, but, boy, were there a lot of double-takes! Everybody's a fan of *Star Wars* and *Indiana Jones*. But he was so cool, people didn't hound him or anything. At any rate, Harrison's companion was supposedly pretty knowledgeable about guitars, and he was going to help Harrison pick out a gift for someone else.

They took their time and played numerous guitars. I remember pulling out many flat-top acoustic Gibsons, as well as a number of electric hollowbody and thin hollowbody Gibsons. As usual, there was an "embarrassment of riches" in the store. After about an hour of searching, the man with Harrison concluded that his favorite was a very clean mid-1960s cherry Gibson ES-345 Stereo. He told Harrison that the 345 was outstanding, and he felt strongly about recommending that guitar as a gift for Harrison's friend.

Harrison pulled out his credit card and paid for the guitar. He said to his companion, "Go ahead and put that in your car."

The guy replied, "What do you mean, put it in my car?"

Harrison said, "The gift was for you!"

The man was completely blown away and could not believe that he was receiving such a wonderful gift. Everybody in the store was knocked out. Harrison then explained to me that his friend was his flight instructor and that he wanted to get him a very special gift.

Recently Harrison was in a terrible plane accident flying over Venice, California, in a vintage airplane. He was hurt pretty badly, but he escaped with his life and is now thriving. According to all reports, the reason Harrison survived was because he is an expert pilot and was very well trained. I guess that special gift really paid off! Talk about a crucial investment in friendship. You just never know what the future might bring, especially if you're a few thousand feet up in the air.

That day I reminded Harrison that back in the seventies my band, the Angel City Rhythm Band, used to play at a club in Calabasas called the Sundance Saloon. The club was owned by a nice lady named Helen, who loved us and booked us there fairly regularly. Harrison's eyes lit up. He certainly remembered the Sundance and those "great old days." I don't know if he recalled my band specifically, but he was very gracious about it all.

Two characters who used to hang out at the Sundance were "Teddy Jack Eddy," whose real name is Gary Busey and who later starred in the *Buddy Holly Story*, as well as graced the front pages of countless tabloid stories, and "Harrison the carpenter," which is Harrison Ford. In LA, you never know which future star might be hanging around at your local bar, so remember, "It's nice to be important, but it's more important to be nice!"

———

I have found that if you do a friend a "solid," it often comes back in positive ways. In 1983, my friend J.J. Cale and his girlfriend, guitarist Christine Lakeland, pulled up in his huge tour bus/motor home. They could barely find a place to park it outside the store! Like most musicians of the era, J.J. was in search of Les Paul Sunburst Standards. At the time, I had a couple. The one that spoke to him was a 1960 that had the thinner neck profile. The guitar had a really nice top and was in very good condition.

I always loved J.J.'s playing and writing, and really responded to his low-key manner and how down-to-earth he was. He was a man who didn't care much about money and all the success he'd had as a songwriter. He just wanted to do his thing. Because I liked him so much, I gave J.J. an excellent deal on the axe. I believe it was under $10,000. He ended up using the guitar for about seventeen years, playing it live, but mostly for recording, mainly at his home studio.

In the year 2000, J.J. called and said that he just had too many gui-

Norman and J.J. Cale with a 1960 Gibson Les Paul Sunburst Standard flame top. (Photo by Marlene Harris)

tars! He asked if I was interested in some of them, including the Les Paul. He said he wasn't using it very much anymore. He knew it had gone way up in value, but he wanted to simplify a bit and lighten his load. We made a deal on the instrument, and he was very happy because he received a huge return on his investment.

I kept the guitar for several years and my friend Bob Spector from the bay area came in one day, inquiring about early Gibson Les Paul Sunburst Standards. I showed him the "J.J. Burst" and he was knocked out. He loved the guitar and dug its provenance, because he was a huge J.J. fan, like all of us. Of course, he bought it from me.

I believe Bob eventually sold the guitar and did well with it too. Bob said he knows the whereabouts of the guitar and feels it's in the family of friends. The "J.J. Burst" is one of those special guitars that has it all, including the mojo of being owned and played by J.J. Cale.

J.J. and I remained good friends up until his untimely death a couple years ago. He lived a simple life and felt he did not need a lot of things to make him happy. A well-known recluse, J.J. had agreed to perform at a benefit I organized for The Midnight Mission, but he passed away before the event. I had some ideas about getting him back together with his old Sunburst Les Paul for "one night only," but sadly, it was not meant to be.

J.J. was such a good-hearted and generous man. While we were going through his guitars, he pointed to a few in the corner of his living room and said, "Why don't we give these to The Midnight Mission?" The folks at the Mission raised quite a bit of money when they sold J.J.'s guitars and are forever grateful. Rest in peace, my old friend.

29

A
MISSION

O ne Christmas morning, I was watching the news on TV, and they showed all these kids lining up for toys at The Midnight Mission in downtown LA. I said to myself, "Next Christmas, I'm going to rent a truck, buy a ton of toys, and drop them off there."

The next Christmas I did just that. There was a lady who worked at Mattel who used to come into the store, and she helped me get a lot of toys wholesale, and I rented a truck and went down there.

The first person I met was Orlando Ward, who had once been a star basketball player at Stanford before a long battle with drugs took him to skid row, and finally, to the Mission, where he got his life together. I was going to drop off the toys, and he said to me, "We have this place called Santa's Village over there. Why don't you give out the toys to the kids, instead of just dropping them off?"

I'm Jewish. I don't really celebrate Christmas, but it was a powerful and emotional experience seeing the kids and families there, who have to rely on the Mission for basic necessities, like a hot meal. It was heartbreaking to see, but I was incredibly moved. My small involvement was what us Jews might call a "mitzvah."

That was twelve years ago. I started getting involved with them because I saw some of the people doing great work there, and I asked how I could help. Well, distributing toys was one thing, but like every organization involved in that world, they needed funds. I got an idea—maybe I could raise some money by getting some of the musicians I know to put on a concert. But I wasn't sure that these stars I'd done business with would be interested in something like that.

—————

The first person I asked to play was Richie Sambora, and without a second's hesitation, he said, "I'm in!" I was taken aback. I didn't think he'd be so receptive, and it built my confidence.

So, next thing I knew, we had lined up Jackson Browne, Los Lobos, the Zen Cruisers, (which was Doug Fieger from the Knack; Elliot Easton from the Cars; Teddy Andreadis, keyboardist for Guns N' Roses; and Clem Burke from Blondie), Freebo, and Ilsey Juber (the great Laurence Juber's daughter) for a fundraising concert for The Midnight Mission.

"From Hollywood with Love," The Midnight Mission Benefit Concert. Backstage with Jimmy Vivino, Joe Bonamassa, Orianthi, Richie Sambora, and Norman Harris. (Photo by Jen Angkahan)

Previously my friend Tony Berg had gotten me to set up a little bou-
tique store at the five-hundred-seat Malibu Performing Arts Center,
which was also a state-of-the-art recording concert hall, so that was
naturally the place to do the show. Richie hosted, as well as played, and
we did very well with it.

So I figured, let's keep going, and I asked my old friend, the legendary John Mayall, to perform a set, and we put him on the bill with REO
Speedwagon, my old bandmate Rick Vito, and Laurence Juber.

The third show was the one I mentioned in a previous chapter, with
Tom Petty reuniting Mudcrutch for what was supposed to be one night
only. It was hosted by my old friend and NBC weather forecaster Fritz
Coleman. I had used that Rickenbacker Rose Morris as bait, so Tom
was happy to trade his services and some memorabilia for doing this
show. It was the first time they'd played in thirty years, and they ending up cutting another record and going out on tour after that, so it was
very cool.

Over the years, I've hit up a lot of my friends and acquaintances
to perform at fund raisers for The Midnight Mission, including Don
Felder from the Eagles, another one of my bandmates Bobby Caldwell,
the great Robben Ford, Orianthi, Jimmy Vivino, Jimmy Earl, Joe Bonamassa, Richie Sambora, Tony Galla, Kirk Fletcher, John Jorgenson,
Grant Geissman, Del Casher, and Kevin Nealon from *Saturday Night
Live*.

I've almost become a professional beggar, asking all of these musicians to play for no pay, but if you don't ask, it's never going to happen.
Sometimes it can be a little uncomfortable, but I know it's for a good
cause. The Midnight Mission is a special place, because it really tries
to help rehabilitate people and get them back on their feet, educated,
and into the workforce, among other things. There's no religious com-
ponent either, which is unusual.

=====

After forty years hanging around the music business, I've seen, heard, and even played with some extraordinary talent—talent that most people have never even heard of.

Lenny Breau was a breathtaking guitarist; a child prodigy who evolved out of country music into one of the most highly respected jazz guitarists of all time. He invented his own seven-string guitar with a high A string, so he could play chords and improvise at the same time. He was utterly unique and one of the guitar players I knew Ted Greene loved and respected. Ted would see him play out over and over again and do anything to help him.

Before Lenny's untimely murder in 1984, at the age of 43, he did a gig at Donte's jazz club in the valley. Ted insisted we go together. He was nothing short of astounding. He had it all—taste, technique, and swing. After the show, Ted introduced me to Lenny, who looked to me like a character out of a Toulouse-Lautrec painting. When I told him how knocked out I was by his playing, he said only one thing to me . . .

"Got any acid?"

=====

Another guy who'll always stick with me is Ronnie Barron—the heaviest New Orleans–style piano player I've ever seen, direct from the school of Professor Longhair. He had it all: talent, musicality, and funk. The first time I saw him was on TV playing Hammond B3 with Paul Butterfield in a band called Better Days. I'll never forget, he was playing this tune called "I Broke My Baby's Heart." He started singing down real low in the bass register, and after working his way through the octaves, he was up in the stratosphere singing falsetto. The range and quality of his voice was so extraordinary, I was blown away.

Later, Rick Vito mentioned him in passing, and I told him I had to meet him, and we ended up becoming friends. I hung out with him as much as I could. Ronnie could sit down at the piano or organ and sing anything. He knew all of those New Orleans tunes, because he was the real thing. In fact, he was so multitalented that the arranger Don Costa, when inventing the concept of Dr. John the Night Tripper originally pegged Ronnie to play the character that Mac Rebennack became so famously identified as.

Success was not meant to be with Ronnie. He was one of those guys, like Jaco, who became his own worst enemy. At one point, the Rolling Stones wanted him to join the group, but he blew that opportunity, too. It was a self-fulfilling prophecy—he couldn't deal with success. He'd rather burn the house down than embrace moving forward in his life. He had a lot of baggage and did a lot of drugs, and just had a real "living problem."

He didn't die of an OD or anything, but I knew the booze and the drugs had done their thing with him—that slow, inexorable diminishment. Last time I saw him, he had been taking cortisone so long, his head was entirely inflated. He pretended that things were okay, but we all knew it was only a matter time and he soon would be dead. He was 54.

Both Lenny and Ronnie were two of the finest musicians I've ever seen. But in almost every other aspect of their lives, their ability to thrive and survive was a disaster. When I was young, I did a lot of stupid stuff, taking drugs, as you know. I was involved in many of the same activities as Lenny and Ronnie, and countless others. I often wonder, why not me? Why was I not a casualty, like those guys? Why did I survive to have a family and run a business, while these others, more talented than I, got on the path to heartbreak and oblivion? It's a mystery that I will never solve. I know in my heart of hearts, it's only a matter of grace that I was able to build a life, instead of self-destructing or ending up on the streets. I have personally seen so much destruction caused by drugs. Sometimes wisdom is acquired by living a long life and going through a lot.

═══════

The face of the homeless has changed in the last decade. Many families are now at the Mission, as a result of bad luck during the recession of 2008. But the majority are people who have that "living problem," which is hastened by drug abuse and alcoholism. The Midnight Mission is an exceptional example of an institution trying to help these folks with all aspects of that problem.

One dream I have always had is to do a series of concerts as Homeless Aid (like Live Aid). I believe homelessness to be one of our biggest domestic problems. If any of my friends and customers are reading this, I would love their help in organizing such an event.

30

SHAKING ALL OVER

J anuary 17, 1994, is a day I will never forget. I had moved to Calabasas in 1992, and we had been renovating our new house. At 4:30
a.m., Marlene and I were woken up by an enormous jolt. It honestly felt
like a plane had just landed on the roof! I knew immediately that we'd
been through a very strong earthquake. I had been in several smaller
quakes, and sometimes it feels like a gentle roll or maybe like a sledge-
hammer's banging. This one was very sharp and intense. Marlene and
I gathered the kids and made our way to a safe area in the house. We
were pretty disoriented but glad to be alive.

I've talked to some native Angelinos who aren't fazed by earthquakes, no matter how big. Because I am from Florida, it's a whole
other story. In the back of my mind, I'm always wondering when the
"Big One" is going to hit.

Earthquakes are usually followed by aftershocks, and this one was
no exception. After a few more sporadic jolts, the shaking subsided.
We all looked at each other, and the first thing I said was, "At least we
are okay." Marlene definitely was shaken up, but my kids (those native
Angelinos) were just psyched for the adventure. They wanted more!

There was some damage around the house, and we quickly went
from room to room to see how badly we were hit. We turned on the TV
to find out where the epicenter was. The newsman said Northridge.

CONFESSIONS OF A VINTAGE GUITAR DEALER

Norman's Rare Guitars, 1992 earthquake, at 6753 Tampa Avenue, Reseda, California. (Photo by Marlene Harris)

My store at the time was in Reseda, which is the next adjacent suburb. In other words, we were really close, and it certainly felt like it. I told Marlene to watch the kids while I jumped in the car and headed toward the store.

It was still dark outside, and as I made my way closer and closer to the store, it was surreal. The devastation became more and more obvious. It looked like a war zone. Houses were heavily damaged. Brick walls had come down, and there were bricks and debris all over the place. I had to drive very slowly to avoid some huge potholes that had opened up. With every block, the damage seemed more severe. What was strange was that on some sides of the streets the damage was horrible, while the other side looked totally unmarred.

When I arrived at the store, I braced myself for the worst. Everything in the area looked torn apart. My store sat at the corner of Tampa and Vanowen. The Tampa side was a disaster, but the Vanowen side did not look that bad at all. I could see through the window on the Vanowen side that a lot of guitars had fallen out of the hooks on the wall. We had

Norman's Rare Guitars, 1992 earthquake, at 6753 Tampa Avenue, Reseda, California. (Photo by Marlene Harris)

a raised area almost like a stage that displayed some guitars. Most had fallen out of their stands. We sustained quite a bit of damage, but to my surprise many of our instruments that had fallen over only sustained minimum damage.

There was a young man who used to come by and wash our cars named Todd Lee. He was a good guy but had a very serious drug problem. We liked him, but we were very aware of his problem and couldn't trust him completely. So, it was really cool that he noticed one of our windows was broken and pulled up a chair to guard our store against any looters. Sometimes even though a man has serious problems, his true character still shines through. He loved the store, and to my amazement offered us protection until I arrived. Whenever a situation like a natural disaster happens, some opportunists try to take advantage of the chaos.

Most of our high-end guitars were in cases in the back, and none of these guitars sustained any damage at all. I tried to take care of our most immediate problems, including boarding up our doors and windows. When I finally recovered most of my senses, another thought dawned on me. What about my warehouse? I had quite a large personal collection housed in Beverly Hills Moving and Storage in Sherman Oaks, about five miles east of the store.

I immediately jumped in the car to get to the warehouse and assess whatever damage may have occurred. When I got there, numerous police and fire trucks were already at the location. My heart sank. Yellow tape had been posted around the entire warehouse. I asked the police if I could go inside and check to see if my instruments, which were in large wooden containers, were okay. I was told nobody was allowed to enter.

I asked when I would be able to go in and check. The police said, "Possibly at a later date, or possibly never!" It was too dangerous to go inside, they said.

Later date! I called every day for three months, and each time I never received a positive answer.

Those three months were agony. Whatever insurance I had wouldn't cover the actual value of many of my priceless, irreplaceable guitars. I figured I could be completely wiped out. Finally, I received a call saying that the warehouse was now safe to enter. I still was nervous thinking that I was about to see something really bad. Miraculously, when I went in, all my storage bins were intact, and there was no damage to any of the guitars. They had been packed that well, in the bins.

I must be one of the luckiest guys alive! Because all of the instruments were in hard cases, and the cases were in wooden storage pallets, everything was well protected.

So, I dodged a bullet. I'm pretty prepared for the next one. Please let it not be the "Big One."

31

YOU CAN'T
DO IT ALONE

B eing located in Los Angeles, I have been exposed to some of the
biggest names in the music business. So many of these people
have by word of mouth, helped me to get established in the vintage guitar business. Tom Petty, Richie Sambora, Dave Amato, John 5, Robbie
Robertson, George Harrison, and so many more recommended me to
their friends. I believe word of mouth is always the finest endorsement.

In my early days in Miami, band members Bobby Caldwell and
Bobby Jabo hipped me to the differences between vintage guitars and
guitars that were currently being made. Mr. John Black and G. L. Styles
were the go-to repairman. They took the time to answer my questions
and arm me with a little knowledge about vintage guitars. When I arrived in LA, Milt Owens did the same. All these folks recommended me
to their friends and colleagues. This helped me in getting established,
and it created a customer base.

If I have left anyone out, please forgive me. I will always be grateful
for all the help I have received, and as anyone knows, you just can't do
it alone.

―――――

When it comes to technical stuff, I guess you would say I'm a techno-
phobe. I resisted being on the Internet for as long as humanly pos-

The whole gang from Norman's Rare Guitars, 18969 Ventura Boulevard, Tarzana, California. (Photo by Jen Angkahan)

sible. My son, Jordan, and my daughter, Sarah, live on the computer. My daughter has her own search engine optimization company. They both said I was a dinosaur, and I needed to get with it and give the store a large Internet presence, as well as develop our social media. I fought it, like a stubborn old mule.

Finally, I have to admit, I was wrong! Since developing our social media, business has improved remarkably. It also has given our international customers immediate access to our latest acquisitions. Our videos are approaching twenty million hits, and our subscriber base on our YouTube channel continues to grow by leaps and bounds. We also started doing videos of our celebrity customers, as well as young and up-and-coming talents. We also have done informational videos, as well as videos showing the usual hijinks that go on at the store. I had no idea how many people would be interested in our everyday goings-on here, but they are. My son, Jordan, has developed an Instagram following that is truly astounding. Thousands of people watch his every post and are interested in all of our latest acquisitions. The interest in these things is amazing to me.

To get with it, in the modern era, I've learned to trust the "natives." By that, I mean the young people who have come of age during the computer era. Now with our store manager, Mark Agnesi, who is very Internet savvy, and also with Jen Angkahan, who handles the day-to-day Internet, Facebook, Twitter, and photography for the store, my son, Jordan, doing the social media, and my daughter, Sarah, optimizing our website, I have to say things have really changed. Our profile is bigger than ever. We have even been recognized by NAMM (National Association of Musical Merchants) for our Internet presence.

Hosting our videos, we rotate between myself, Jordan, Mark, and Nick Dias. There are always some colorful characters in the store, including our talented luthier Joel Whitehead AKA "Ringo" and John Tucci, who does our tube amp and guitar repairs. Jen does all the editing and photography for our website and videos, and I believe we have an excellent team. We try to make the videos as much fun as possible, as well as adding some information along the way. I can honestly say, I never would have done any of it without the persistent badgering of my kids, and the kids who work with me, and I am very grateful to them for it.

Conclusion

WISDOM

Last year I was asked by the Musician's Institute to deliver a commencement address for their graduating class. It provided an opportunity for me to reflect upon the music business, my role in it, and how I got here.

When I look back, I see the two sides of my upbringing coming together in my life: the love my father had for music and his business acumen. I was able to fuse the passion for one with the instinct and drive of the other. I have been inordinately lucky. So many people more talented than I have been casualties of the lifestyle that often seems to go with music.

I remember when I was a young man being visited by the encyclopedia salesmen. In their trunks were twenty-six large books, the sum "knowledge" of our culture, which would become obsolete every few years. Needless to say, the world has changed drastically. Now with the push of a button on a computer, you can find the latest information on anything in the world instantaneously.

The music world also looks very different from the one I tried to break into fifty years ago. It's pretty hilarious to see how primitive it all was back then. I have lived through the period of deep transition from hit radio and singles to the Album Oriented Rock format, LPs to

CDs, MP3s, file sharing, and the crisis of the big music companies. Income drivers like publishing rights and protection of intellectual property have gone away. Everything seems to be in flux. That's why it's important to be flexible, whatever you pursue, to be able to roll with all the punches that come.

———

I reminded the graduates of MI that I was not a great student, and I stayed in school only to avoid the draft. I have limited abilities in many aspects of life. Like my old buddy Dan Duehren says, "Norm couldn't pour piss out of a boot if the instructions were written on the heel!"

What I did do was find something I loved and carved out a business from it. That was my main message—find something you love, and then put all your effort into it. Put in your hours and your time. Most of what I learned came from a practical, hands-on approach. Nothing teaches better than actual experience and years of doing one thing.

Having that drive is an important part of success, I believe. You have to be decisive, and strike while the iron is hot. If any guitars came my way, I was going to land them! Fifty years later, I still am willing to get out of bed and drive at two in the morning, if it means I'll have first crack at something great. I still get a rush from it. My joy is in the buying, not the selling. The selling just fuels my buying, in the end.

On the flipside, nothing stalls out more in life than procrastination. My business has born that out, because if you don't show up with the money and are not willing to step up, you could lose that once-in-a-lifetime guitar. You need to know your product and be ready to make a deal.

My business is unusual, because it's one of the only ones that can grow, even if your inventory isn't moving. Any other business would have to fold up if things aren't selling. In fact, it's crazy because the longer I've held on to some instruments, the more valuable they've become.

Also, because I was a stickler for originality and condition back when nobody cared about that, I was just a little ahead of my time. Guitars transitioned from mere tools of the trade to collectible classics. People thought I was nuts when I was willing to pay more for an old guitar than a new one, but they turned out to be a great investment.

I have inadvertently become a protector of vintage guitars. Many of the guitars in my collection have become a reference point for Fender and Gibson when they want to build reissues. Incredibly, nobody really knew what Fender "sonic blue" actually looked like, because lacquer and exposure to air changes a guitar's color over time. Luckily, I was able to help Fender out, because I had some pristine examples in my collection.

———

I firmly believe, even though there are many fine guitars being built today, that nothing will ever equal the great guitars of the past. The materials just do not exist anymore. There is no more old-growth Adirondack spruce, rosewood, or the same alloys and metals used in guitar pickups. There are no more old artisans who worked in the guitar factory, carving and tap-tuning archtops like there used to be.

On the surface, many reissues might look the same as the originals, but there is a difference. They can never be truly duplicated, because the old guitars represent the traditional know-how that existed back then, before computer technology entered the picture. Each guitar had its own individual footprint.

———

People often ask me if I see any recent technological innovations in guitar making. Aside from a few things like clip-on tuners, little has been added to guitars that is an improvement over everything that's come before. That holds as true today as it did fifty years ago. I can point to the tune-o-matic bridge, the cutaway, and the humbucking pickup as designs that really enhanced the utility of guitars, but they've been around for decades.

We're in an age of incredible technological leaps. Music can practically be made without any live musicians. I've been to more and more performances where people sing to prerecorded tracks, and the audience doesn't seem to notice any difference. To me, this artificial perfection lacks soul, as well as the spontaneity that can arise during live creation with real musicians.

The good news is musicians have become a lot more serious about their art and craft, thankfully. Someone like Joe Bonamassa, who I've known since he was twelve years old, epitomizes the new professionalism of the breed. All those old blues musicians I played with were content to grind it out on the road in small clubs and were barely able to survive. Joe has a focus and purpose to his career, is approachable and talented, and as a result, it has taken off. He certainly deserves all his success.

Musicians today are more practical. They have to be. Gone are the excesses of living high on the hog, the limos, and the multiple wives (for the most part!). Young musicians today have a past history to learn from. They understand that a career doesn't go on forever. Eventually, the ride will end, unless your band's name is the Rolling Stones.

I know much of my story involved drugs, and I want to make it clear, I don't condone that behavior. I'm just trying to keep it real. With age, I can now see how destructive drugs were, on so many levels. Using drugs truly is "playing with fire," and I was lucky I didn't get burned.

The truth is, every generation has to rebel. Even if the young listeners seem to be into more processed electronic music, the pendulum will swing back eventually. The guitar will always have its rightful place in composing and performing.

Unfortunately, the price of fine vintage instruments seems to be out of the hands of your regular players these days. But once anybody feels and hears the difference, there is no going back. It's kind of like driving a Chevy versus a Mercedes. The Chevy will transport you well enough, and you'll get to where you're going, but the ride doesn't compare to the exhilaration you get from driving a Mercedes.

Still, in the end it's all about the music. That's how I got into it—I loved music, and I wanted to get my hands on the best tools possible to make music. In the final analysis, it'll always be about some young man or woman sitting down, strumming some crisp chords on an acoustic guitar, or plugging an electric guitar into a tube amp, and playing something that speaks to them and other people. I never forget that it's about the joy of creating music.

———

Thank you for taking the time to read my story. I wish all of you peace, love, and good health.

Index

Les Paul Standard Sunburst (1959), 74–75, 96
Les Paul Sunburst, xiii, 92, 95–96, 124–27, *125*, 129–30, 132
Melody Maker pickups and, 69
with one-offs, 142–44
ownership changes of, 135–36
P-90 pickups on, 70, 74, 94, 109–10, 164
Premiere designation for Cutaway, 13
Ray Corrigan SJ 100/200 (1937), 57–62, *58*
Rosewood J-200 (1940), 103, *105*, 106, 108
SG Special, 93–94
status and value of 'Burst, 109–14
Gibson Sunburst (1958-1960) guitar ('Burst)
Harris, N., and Les Paul guitars, 109–14, *111*
Les Paul left-handed guitar, 112–14, *113*
gigs, 44–47, 78–79, 82–83
"Give Me Love," 38
"Give Me That Wine," 140
Glenwood, National (1964), *184*, 184–85
Glick, Richard, 72–74, 107
goals, musician's, x
Gold Dust Twins, 11
Grady, June, *174*
Grady, Kyle, *174*, 174–76, *176*
Gray, Dobie, 78
"Grease," 22
Greene, Ted, *145*, 146–50, *150*, 200
Gregg Allman Band, xiii–xiv

Gretsch guitars, 40–41, 71, 103, 107–8
grievances, 16
Gruber, Kenny, 10
Guest, Chris, 72–76
Guitar Center, 33
guitar god hustle, 124–27
guitar industry, xiv, 177–79
Guitar Player, 152
guitars. *See also specific guitars*
archtop, 13, 103, *116*, 116–17, 136–37, 139, 213
collectors of, 132–34
cowboys' popularity with, 57–62, 102–3
earthquake damage to, 204–6
Ford purchasing, 191–93
forgery, 190
fulfillment of dreams and, x–xi
Hollywood and period correct, 63–66, 70
mono and stereo, 143
one-offs and mysterious, 135–44
period correct, 65
priceless, 206
repair of, 209
seventies' bad reputation for, xix
shops for, xv–xvi
shows for, xx–xxii
steel, 86, 89
technological innovations in, 213–14
Western, 57–62
"guitar safaris," xv
The Guitar Shoppe, 33
Guitar's R Us, 54
Guitar World, 152–53
Guthrie, Woody, 65